P9-CAN-930

CALIFORNIA
C·O·O·K·I·N·G

by Mable & Gar Hoffman

HPBooks

Mable & Gar Hoffman

Mable and Gar Hoffman have lived in California most of their lives. Together, they form Hoffman Food Consultants, a partnership which specializes in consulting for California food industries, food styling for photographic work, recipe development and writing. The Hoffmans' personal and professional interest is California foods. They are also interested in the ways Californians prepare food. Both enjoy traveling, and do so frequently in California as well as throughout the world.

Books written by the Hoffmans include *Appetizers, Chocolate Cookery, Crepe Cookery, Crockery Cookery, Deep-Fry Cookery* and *Ice Cream*. Their books have won four Tastemaker Awards, the "Oscar" for cookbooks, as best soft-cover cookbook of the year. Two of their books have appeared on the *New York Times* best-seller list.

They enjoy preparing new and exciting dishes and sharing them with family and friends. In this book, they share some of the California cuisine they have enjoyed so long. ❖

C·O·N·T·E·N·T·S

ANOTHER BEST-SELLING VOLUME FROM HPBOOKS

Publishers: Bill and Helen Fisher; Executive Editor: Rick Bailey;
Editorial Director: Helen Fisher; Editor: Retha M. Davis;
Art Director: Don Burton; Book Design: Dana Martin;
Food Stylist: Mable Hoffman;
Photography: George de Gennaro Studios—George de Gennaro,
Tom Miyasaki, Dennis Skinner, David Wong

Special thanks to the Wine Institute for the California wine labels.

Published by HPBooks
P.O. Box 5367, Tucson, AZ 85703
602/888-2150
ISBN 0-89586-236-0
Library of Congress Catalog Card Number 83-80598
© 1983 Fisher Publishing, Inc. Printed in the U.S.A.

COVER PHOTO: Golden State Avocado Boats, page 112.

The backyard barbecue shown on the previous pages includes Teriyaki Pinwheels, page 99; Skewered Sourdough Cubes, page 105; Cheese-Stuffed Tomatoes and Barbecued Squash, page 108.

California Cooking

California cooking was spawned years ago by hardy pioneers who trekked thousands of miles over hot, dusty plains and lofty mountains. Their ability to acquire game and other foods and to make them palatable under primitive conditions is a tribute to their resourcefulness and ingenuity. Much of this spirit prevails today, but fortunately without life-threatening aspects.

CALIFORNIA'S BOUNTY

Abundance and availability of an incredible array of fresh ingredients is the greatest single contribution to California's culinary achievement. Where else in the United States can you find locally grown artichokes, citrus, dates, garlic, kiwi and walnuts—to name a few? California ranks first in the United States in the production of such crops as almonds, apricots, artichokes, broccoli, cauliflower, celery, dates, figs, garlic, kiwi, nectarines, olives, peaches, plums, tomatoes and the list goes on.

California cooks have taken advantage of all these assets. They have an almost fanatical fetish for acquiring fruits and vegetables at the peak of perfection. They know the freshest ingredients impart maximum flavor. Local markets are aware of these desires and make every effort to provide ingredients to satisfy customers' demands. Grower-operated fruit and vegetable stands also abound in the state to help meet this need.

GREAT EXPERIMENTERS

Californians are incurable experimenters and are highly motivated to learn from others. Over the years, many diverse ethnic groups have beaten a path to California. These groups have intermingled educationally, professionally and socially. Each has borrowed and changed the other's cuisine, resulting in a flavor more pleasing to the borrower's taste. Thus, it is very common to find a dozen variations of a classic ethnic dish. It is not unusual to observe 50 or more cookbooks in a serious cook's library. These same people clamor for the opportunity to attend cooking classes. Although they shop supermarkets for their basic needs, they also browse gourmet shops seeking exotic ingredients and unique culinary equipment.

NEW-WAVE CUISINE

In recent years, California has seen an influx of young, truly creative chefs. They have opened their doors in secluded landscapes, as well as large cities. Their innovative approach to cooking is creating what we call California's *New-Wave Cuisine*. These chefs produce fascinating culinary creations that are setting national cooking trends. They have been largely responsible for the development and in-state production of specialized and exotic products that were previously available only as imports. These products include California Brie and goat cheese, domestic caviar, smoked duck and others.

In their search for absolute freshness, the chefs are going directly to the source, whether it be grower, cheesemaker, rancher or fisherman. And, a grateful clientele is beating a path to these new-wave restaurants. Patrons are anxious to try many of the new creations in their own kitchens. For this reason, we have included our interpretations of some of these popular innovations.

We hope *California Cooking* will help you get to know and appreciate the creative cuisine of California. No matter where you live, you will find the flavorful healthy dishes of a bountiful state can be served and enjoyed at your own table.❖

Cook's Tour

To acquaint yourself with some of the more prominent ingredients used in California cooking, refer to the following food glossary. Fruits, vegetables and nuts are very abundant. Cooks in California take for granted their year-round availability. They may not be as readily available in all parts of the country. Mexican foods are also closely associated with California cooking.

ALMONDS
California's central valley is one of the most important almond-producing areas in the world. During the fall and winter, buy almonds in the shell or shelled. As weather gets warmer, only shelled almonds are available. One pound of unshelled almonds yields slightly more than a cup of shelled almonds. Unfortunately, the high fat content encourages rancidity. Store shelled or unshelled nuts in airtight containers in your refrigerator or freezer.

APPLES
Although California may not be thought of as a major apple-producing area, it ranks fourth nationally. Apples are available fresh as well as in a variety of processed forms. With improved storage, the quality of apples is good year round. A large percentage of California's Gravenstein apples is used for making applesauce.

APRICOTS
California's climate is especially agreeable to apricot production. During June and July, fresh apricots are shipped to many parts of the world. Apricots should be an orange-gold color with a reddish blush and a velvety feel. Avoid greenish-yellow or dull-looking fruit. Unfortunately, apricot season is short, so the rest of the year you must depend on dried or canned apricots.

ARTICHOKES
Rich soil combines with early morning fog and hot afternoon sun to make the Castroville area perfect for growing artichokes. Most artichokes are shipped fresh to markets throughout the year When buying fresh artichokes, choose those with firm solid heads, compact leaves and a fresh-green color. During winter, you'll see an occasional bronze touch on the leaf tips. These artichokes are *winter-kissed*. The color is caused by frost or cold weather. It does not adversely affect the quality. Hearts are available in frozen packages. Artichoke hearts and bottoms packed in jars or cans are either marinated or water-packed.

ASPARAGUS
Fresh asparagus is a symbol of spring. When buying asparagus, look for tightly closed tips and firm stalks. Because asparagus is very perishable, plan to use it as soon as possible. If you can't use it immediately, wrap the stalk ends in a moist paper towel. Store in your refrigerator.

AVOCADO
Avocados are native to the New World and date back to the Aztec civilization. The winter variety, known as *Fuerte*, has a thin skin, pear shape and deep-green color. *Hass* is the best-known summer variety. It is usually wider and shorter than Fuerte. When ripe, it has a black pebbled skin with the same light yellow-green velvety texture inside.

Avocados are ready to eat if they yield to gentle pressure. If they aren't soft when you buy them, keep them at room temperature for several days. They will ripen on the counter, in a brown-paper bag or in a ripening bowl.

For recipes where avocado is mashed, use the softest fruit. Sprinkle cut surfaces of avocado with lemon juice to delay browning.

BEANS—LIMA & SNAP
Over 50% of the nation's lima-bean supply comes from California. The state also produces about 12% of the fresh-market supply of snap beans. Both types are grown in the lower San Joaquin Valley and central coast area. Fresh, frozen or canned beans are always a tasty treat.

BRIE CHEESE

One of the most famous French cheeses, Brie, is now made in California. It is round with a flat top. The creamy-white inside is coated with a soft white to light-brown edible crust. Each package is dated to indicate when it should be used. Six to eight weeks before the date, the cheese is mild and firm. Four to six weeks before the date, it is partially ripened. Three weeks until the deadline, it is fully ripened. *Ripened* means stronger in flavor and softer in texture. For best flavor, remove Brie from refrigerator two to three hours before serving.

BROCCOLI

This popular, nutritious vegetable is used in many California dishes. It's available year round. When buying, look for firm stalks and dark-green tightly closed buds. Divide thick stalks into quarters by cutting slits through the bottom. Cook in a small amount of water or steam until tender. Broccoli is also delicious raw.

BRUSSELS SPROUTS

Brussels sprouts are a small unusual vegetable which look like miniature cabbages. They grow close together on tall single-stem stalks. They are great for freezing. To assure even cooking, make two diagonal cuts in the base of each sprout. Cook by steaming or in boiling water.

CARROTS

Versatile and colorful carrots are important in making salads, soups, sauces and side dishes. Markets sell them with or without tops. Look for small firm carrots. Avoid cracked or limp rubbery ones. Carrots are not as perishable as many other vegetables, but have best flavor and nutrition when eaten soon after buying. They are usually the most popular item on a raw-vegetable tray.

CAULIFLOWER

Cauliflower is in continuous production in the central and southern coastal areas of California. That assures consumers of a fresh supply year round and supplies large volumes to the processing industry. California produces over 75% of the nation's supply. Cauliflower is a popular vegetable, especially eaten raw with dips.

CELERY

Celery is available throughout the year. Over 70% of the nation's supply comes from California, particularly the central and southern coastal areas. Choose a firm bunch with crisp stalks. Celery is great served raw with a dip or stuffed with cheese. Its flavor enhances a variety of cooked dishes and soups.

CELERY ROOT

Also known as *celeriac*, this vegetable is served throughout Europe. Until recently, it was seldom eaten here. Look for a brown root-vegetable with a few green tops and a white interior. Select the smaller size without any sprouts on the root. Peel it like a potato. Keep it in water or sprinkle with lemon juice to retain the white color. Slice or shred to eat raw or cooked. It is a crunchy, delicately flavored addition to a green salad.

CHERRIES, SWEET

During the early summer, in the northern San Joaquin and Santa Clara Valleys, you will see the beautiful sweet-cherry trees full of fresh red fruit. These are the juicy, tasty cherries we all enjoy for the brief time they are in the market. Enjoy a cherry sauce as a topping for roast pork or lamb.

CILANTRO OR CORIANDER

Cilantro or *Chinese Parsley* is a fresh lacy green leaf about the size and color of parsley. It is used in Mexican and Chinese dishes. Select crisp green bunches without wilted or yellow leaves. It is perishable and should be kept in the refrigerator.

CLAMS, PISMO

Digging clams has been a popular pastime for local people and visitors at Pismo Beach. It is so popular that special regulations must be followed. The clam limit is ten per day per person and each clam must be at least 4-1/2 inches wide. These clams are for your own consumption and may not be sold.

CUCUMBERS

Cucumbers are produced both as a fresh market crop and for pickling. They are grown year round in the valley regions of the state. Cucumbers are a favorite fresh item to include in salads and on vegetable trays.

DAIRY PRODUCTS

California, especially San Bernardino County, is a leader in national dairy production. Creative cooks use dairy products in much of their cooking. Of particular interest are sour cream, yogurt and cottage cheese. Sour cream is popular in sauces, salad dressings, desserts and a variety of

Front row, left to right: Avocados, Tangerine, Strawberries, Kiwi and Nectarines
Center row, left to right: Persimmon and Pomegranate
Back row, left to right: Crenshaw Melon, Plums, Honeydew Melon and Grapes

Front row, left to right: Artichoke, Green Peas, Cilantro, Arugula, Asparagus and Jicama
Back row, left to right: Broccoli, Brussels Sprouts, Celery Root and Radicchio

other dishes. Yogurt is used in meat sauces and desserts and is often a substitute for mayonnaise. Cottage cheese is an important food alone or combined with other foods. All dairy products are perishable and should be kept refrigerated.

DATES

Little did people planting date palms in the early 1900s realize the mammoth industry they were starting in the Coachella Valley. Today, the area between Palm Springs and the Salton Sea produces millions of pounds of dates each year. One tree may produce as much as 300 pounds of fruit. *Deqlet Noor* makes up the largest part of the crop. *Medjool*, a large dark date, is in great demand for gift packs. Many people think of dates as dried fruits, but actually they are fresh ripe fruits. The softness, dryness, firmness or length of time they keep depends on the variety. The more popular commercial ones can be kept at room temperature several weeks or refrigerated for months.

FENNEL

Also called *finocchio* or *sweet anise*, this vegetable looks like celery, but has feathery leaves similar to dill. The flavor and aroma are anise, the ever-popular licorice. In cooking, use the greenish-white bulbous part, plus about 1 inch of the stalk. It is delicious raw or cooked.

FIGS

Fresh figs are highly prized because they are available only in the late summer or early fall. They are extremely perishable and should not be kept more than two to three days. Colors range from a mottled beige, light green to dark purple. Make sure figs are ripe when you serve them. To peel or not to peel fresh figs is a matter of personal choice. Dried figs are available year round. They are an excellent source of energy and nutrients.

GARLIC

This essential seasoning is grown in the San Joaquin Valley, Gilroy and Southern California areas. California is the nation's leading supplier. Garlic is available fresh year round as well as in various forms including powder, salt and other garlic-seasoned mixtures. Whole garlic may be baked and served as an appetizer or snack spread. Baking garlic reduces the strong flavor.

GINGER

Fresh gingerroot is a light brown, round root with small appendages that look like toes. It is usually found in the produce department. Remove the peel and grate or slice as much as you need. Store, unwashed, in a perforated plastic bag in refrigerator two to three weeks. Or, freeze in a tightly sealed container. Crystallized ginger is often considered a confection as well as a flavoring. Amber-colored pieces of ginger are coated with crystal-like sugar.

GOAT CHEESE

Always considered a luxury in France, goat cheese is now made in California. Known as *California Chèvre*, it is off-white in color and has an unmistakable piquancy. Leading California restaurants feature this cheese in salads, appetizers or with pasta. Look for it in cheese shops.

GRAPEFRUIT

Grapefruit is a year-round crop. Expect to find honey-colored flesh from grapefruit with bright-yellow skin. The ruby variety has pink flesh with a ruby blush to the skin. Grapefruit may be left at room temperature for a few days, but should be refrigerated when kept longer. Fresh grapefruit is a dieter's delight. Half of a medium grapefruit has only 38 calories, yet contributes more than 50% of the vitamin C recommended for a day.

GRAPES

California supplies more than 90% of the nation's table grapes. Because of the many varieties grown, there is at least one available almost all year. Look for well-colored, plump clusters attached to green pliable stems. Avoid soft or wrinkled grapes. Grapes, both table and wine, are California's most valuable fruit.

JÍCAMA

This unattractive brown root is beginning to be fully appreciated. Peel it like a potato and you'll find a crisp white interior. It's a popular addition to vegetable trays. Crunchy texture makes it welcome in vegetable or chicken salads. It is a good substitute for water chestnuts.

KIWI

This egg-shape fruit with fuzzy-brown skin doesn't look nearly as good as it tastes. A ripe kiwi yields slightly to gentle pressure. Remove the skin and inside is medium-green flesh with small edible seeds. Because kiwi contains an enzyme which prevents gelatin from setting, do not use it in gelatin salads or desserts. Kiwi may be used as a garnish after gelatin is set.

KUMQUATS

These bright-orange miniature citrus grow in many California backyards. You may see them in the market during the winter months. Kumquats make a colorful garnish for poultry or pork roasts. The edible skin is thick and tart. The center has seeds and pulp similar to an orange. Kumquats are also delicious made into sauce.

LEMONS

There's a steady supply of California lemons throughout the year. Unlike any other fruit, they are picked by size and allowed to ripen off the tree in temperature- and humidity-controlled packing houses. Look for lemons with smooth firm skin, free from blemishes and soft spots. Count on one medium lemon for two to three tablespoons lemon juice and one tablespoon grated peel. Recipes in this book requiring lemon juice were tested with fresh lemon juice.

LETTUCE

A number of varieties can be used interchangeably in most recipes. The best known, *iceberg*, has a firm medium-green head. *Romaine* has long narrow stiff leaves that vary from medium green on the outside to light yellow-green in the center. *Boston* lettuce is a loosely packed yellow-green head with short wide leaves. It is quite perishable, so refrigerate it right away. *Bibb* lettuce is similar in shape to Boston, but slightly smaller and more compact. *Salad-bowl* or *leaf* lettuce has leaves clustered loosely around a stem. It does not form an actual head. There is also a variety with reddish-bronze tips. Speciality-produce shops may carry the colorful red lettuce, *radicchio*.

MELONS

Cantaloupe and honeydew melons are grown predominately in California. Over 70% of the nation's supply is produced in the valleys and southern area of the state. Crenshaw melons and watermelons are also grown. Melons are excellent for fruit salads, eating as juicy fruit slices, in tarts or for making juice to be used in beverages and cold soups. Cut and carved, they become delightful containers for fruits or vegetables.

Front row, left to right: Green Chilies, Red and Green Jalapeños, Ripe Olives, Garlic and Rice
Back row, left to right: Flour and Corn Tortillas, Enoki Mushrooms, Champignon de Paris Mushrooms, Tree Oyster Mushrooms, Red Wine, Herb and Plain Goat Cheese and Brie

MONTEREY JACK CHEESE

A creamy pale-yellow color and a semisoft texture are characteristics of this mild cheese. The name came from the man who first marketed this cheese in the Monterey area. It is the traditional cheese used in many Mexican-type recipes and very popular for snacks and sandwiches. Similar to Monterey Jack is *Sonoma Jack* cheese which is made in the Sonoma area.

MUSHROOMS

Mushrooms are grown year round in the cool climate of Monterey and San Francisco. Mushroom caps range in size from 3/4 inch to 3 inches across. Colors vary from white to a creamy beige. Select firm, unbruised caps that are completely closed over the stem. New varieties of mushrooms are being introduced. *Enoki* is known for its very long, slender, creamy stem that is topped with a pinhead button cap. *Shiitake*, a large shallow cap ranging from tan to a light brown, is sold both fresh and dried. *Tree Oyster* mushrooms grow in clusters. They are light on the bottom and darker on the top. All mushrooms are highly perishable. Store in a paper bag in your refrigerator.

NECTARINES

Nectarines, similar in size and color to peaches, have a sweet flavor and distinct aroma. California is the key producer of nectarines, providing over 98% of the nation's crop. Nectarines can be used in pies, tarts, sorbets and fruit salads.

OLIVES

Olive trees growing at the early California missions were important because they produced fruit that was pressed for oil. It was not until the late 19th century that olives took on added value. Then new methods were used to cure and can ripe olives. The smooth dark skin and subtle nut-like flavor was so appealing that ripe olives became a major industry. Olives are used in a variety of dishes as garnishes and just for eating.

ORANGES

These juicy, fresh, versatile fruits are one of California's best contributions to the culinary scene. From November to May, you'll see the *navel orange* which has the characteristic navel formation opposite the stem end. It's known as the *eating orange* because it's easy to peel and seedless. From February through October, the *Valencia* orange is in the markets. It has a slightly thinner skin with a few seeds and is an excellent juice orange. Other varieties are grown in patios and yards in many regions of the state.

PEACHES

From early May into October, fresh California peaches are seen in markets throughout the United States and many other parts of the world. Ripe peaches give to gentle palm pressure and have a fresh creamy or golden color under the bright rosy blush. Avoid those with wrinkles, brown spots or traces of green. If not fully ripened, leave at room temperature in a loosely closed paper bag or in a ripening bowl. Store ripe peaches in the refrigerator. When peeling peaches, sprinkle with ascorbic acid or lemon juice to prevent flesh from darkening.

PEA PODS

Also known as *Snow Peas*, *Chinese Pea Pods* and *Sugar Peas*, this vegetable has become very popular. Pea pods are available fresh or frozen. When buying fresh, look for pods with bright-green color and crisp texture. Do not overcook. If using in a stir-fry recipe, add them last. For salads, blanch them no more than one minute.

PEARS

Pear orchards are one of California's oldest fruit enterprises. Plantings of different varieties were made in the early gold-rush days. *Bartlett* is the most abundant variety. Pears are harvested while still green because they do not ripen on the tree. When you buy pears, place them in a loosely closed paper bag at room temperature or in a ripening bowl. Ripe pears should be stored, unwrapped, in the refrigerator.

PEPPERS—GREEN BELL & CHILI

Many kinds of peppers are available in California. Most common are green bell peppers and chilies. Green bell peppers are commonly used in salads and on raw-vegetable trays. As a flavoring, they blend well with other foods.

Chili peppers vary tremendously in their hotness. When using large amounts of chilies, handle them with gloves to avoid burning your hands. When handling jalapeños or hot chilies, be careful not to touch your eyes or face.

California Green Chilies—Fresh ones are a shiny bright green, about 2 inches across the top and 5 to 7 inches long, tapering to a point. This variety is available canned, whole or diced. It is a mild chili, but expect slight variations.

Jalapeño Chilies—These have a fairly thick dark-green skin and are 2 to 3 inches long. Because they are hot, start with small amounts and taste before you add more. They are also available in cans or bottles.

Crushed Dried Red Peppers—In grocery stores, they are in small jars or cans near the spices and herbs. They are dried small pieces of red peppers and are hot, so go easy.

PERSIMMONS

The most popular persimmon, called *Hachiya*, is shaped like a fig and is a bright, golden-orange color. Before eating, make sure it is soft, ripe and the skin has a translucent look. Persimmons are generally peeled. The pulp will be so soft that you can spoon it out of the skin. Use ripe fruit immediately or store in the freezer in an airtight container. The *Fuyu* variety is reddish-orange and shaped like a tomato. It can be eaten when firmer.

PINE NUTS OR PIÑONS

These are seeds from a pine tree that grows in arid areas. The nuts are creamy colored and about the size of a sunflower seed. Often used in Italian cooking, they are becoming better known in California cuisine. Markets sell them shelled. Toasted, they have a crunchy texture.

PISTACHIOS

Pistachios grow in clusters on a fairly small evergreen tree. These nuts are covered with an off-white or red shell that's usually split at one end. They are seldom sold without the shell. The edible part of a pistachio is a small, oval, pale-green seed-like nut with a dry thin reddish skin. It has a fine texture and distinct flavor and color.

PLUMS & PRUNES

The center of plum production is in the San Joaquin Valley and North Central Coast area. Thanks to more than 140 varieties, fresh-plum season spreads through summer and into the fall. Best known is the *Santa Rosa*, with a purplish-crimson skin and yellow flesh. To ripen plums, keep them at room temperature one to two days. Refrigerate when ripe.

Prune plums are grown predominately in the warm Sacramento Valley. They are a type of European plum with an extra-high sugar content. This permits them to be dried in the sun without fermenting at the pit.

POMEGRANATES

This beautiful autumn fruit is about the size of a large apple. The firm red shell is filled with many seeds coated with juicy crimson pulp. When

Front row, left to right: Dates, Pistachios, Almonds, Pine Nuts and Raisins
Back row, left to right: Walnuts, Sunflower Nuts, Dried Apricots and Dried Figs

buying them, look for a bright-red skin free from cracks. You can eat the whole seeds but most people prefer to eat the pulp or drink juice made from this pulp. Scoop out seeds with a spoon. Then, process the seeds in a blender to extract the juice. Strain to remove seeds.

POTATOES—WHITE & SWEET

Although California ranks only fifth in national potato production, nearly 50% of the winter and spring supply comes from the state. Potatoes are used for the fresh market and for commercial processing. A significant quantity of sweet potatoes is grown in the San Joaquin Valley.

RAISINS

This part of the grape industry is very important in California. Small raisins are made from the *Thompson Seedless* grapes. Larger raisins are made from *Muscat* grapes. Raisins are enjoyed as a nutritious snack and in cooking and baking.

RICE

Throughout the ages, rice has been one of the world's most important foods. In the United States, it was introduced in the late 1600s. Rice is a leading California crop, centering in the Sacramento Valley. California rice is primarily short-grain. When cooked, short-grain rice is tender and moist, with particles tending to cling together.

SPINACH

What could be better in a colorful crisp salad than fresh spinach? California leads the nation in spinach production for both the fresh market and for processing. Spinach salad with a hot, bacon dressing is a favorite on many salad menus. When buying spinach, look for fresh dark-green leaves. Spinach is used in many dishes.

STRAWBERRIES

California produces over 70% of the nation's strawberry crop. Fresh strawberries are available most of the year in California. They are also frozen and used in processed products. When purchasing fresh berries, look for red-ripe, plump berries. In some areas, you can pick your own.

TANGERINES

Tangerines have an easy-to-peel skin and are easy to divide in segments. Each variety has individual characteristics. *Mandarins* have light-orange smooth skins, a mild sweet flavor and few seeds. *Tangelos* are larger and have a tart-sweet flavor. They are a cross between a tangerine and grapefruit. Actual tangerines are the pebble-skin varieties traditional at Christmas time. *Temples* or *Royal Mandarins* are a cross between a tangerine and orange. They are large, red-orange in color and taste similar to an orange. The season ranges from November through May.

TOMATOES

Tomatoes are the number-one vegetable crop in California. Over 75% of the nation's tomatoes are raised in the state. Both fresh-market and processing tomatoes are grown. Tomatoes are canned in a variety of forms including juice, whole, pieces, stewed, sauce and paste. Specialty products include enchilada sauce and salsa.

TORTILLAS

Corn and flour tortillas may be used interchangeably in many recipes. Corn tortillas are preferred for tacos and enchiladas. Burritos and large tostadas use flour tortillas. Both types of tortillas may be homemade or commercially made. Store in the refrigerator or freezer.

WALNUTS

The first California walnut trees were planted by padres in mission yards in the late 1700s. Today, the California walnut crop represents over 70% of the world's supply. Walnuts are popular in cookies, breads, appetizers, cakes and salads. Buy plump, meaty kernels that snap when broken. Store in the original package or sealed plastic bag in your refrigerator or freezer.

WINE

Winemaking in California began when Spanish missionaries established the original missions. The climate makes it possible to grow nearly all wine-grape varieties. Grape production and winemaking increases year after year. There are over 500 wineries in California. Consumer acceptance of California wines has made it one of the state's most important industries.

ZUCCHINI

Zucchini is one of California's most versatile vegetables. It's available year round. Look for tender, small or medium zucchini with a fresh green color. Zucchini is popular as an appetizer. It is also used in soufflés, cakes, breads and cookies.❖

Appetizers

It has been said that first impressions are lasting. If you believe this old saying, you'll agree with Californians that appetizers are a vital part of the cooking scene. Appetizers are the first foods you offer guests and represent a preview of the food to be served.

At one time, California Dip made with dry onion-soup mix and dairy sour cream took California and the rest of the country by storm. In recent times, we have expanded our appetizer horizons to unlimited combinations of food. Ideas are borrowed from many ethnic groups or updated from traditional American recipes.

TODAY'S APPETIZERS

Dips are still very prominent, but they have taken on new personalities. Fresh vegetables are often used. There are several reasons why they have achieved such prominence. First, they are readily available. With more emphasis on diet and health, vegetables provide maximum food value with a minimum of calories. As an added benefit, they are colorful and appetizing. Is it any wonder that your calorie-counting friends will reach for a slivered carrot or zucchini stick with a dab of dip on the end?

Today's hostesses want to enjoy their guests rather than spend the evening in the kitchen. That's why make-ahead appetizers are first choice with everyone. This is especially true if you are having a dinner party. It is important to have the appetizers ready with the exception of last-minute heating or garnishing. Then, you can concentrate on dinner plans. Tuna-Butter Flutes are ideal for this purpose.

At one time, the cost of imported caviar exceeded most budgets. Now, domestic caviar, at a much more reasonable price, is becoming readily available throughout the country. Our Celebration Caviar Spread is an excellent make-ahead recipe featuring domestic caviar.

FUTURE TRENDS

We predict increased popularity of appetizer buffets as a way to entertain. This type of party offers a variety of appetizers—some hot, some cold. It usually includes one or more dips and spreads with vegetables and crackers, fish or poultry appetizers such as Ribbon Salmon Pâté, a hot item like Artichoke-Cheese Wedges and maybe an assortment of cheeses with fresh fruit.

This trend offers a number of advantages. First, you can accommodate more people than at a sit-down dinner. Usually it is easier on the budget. You can choose dishes that can be made ahead. Guests like it because they enjoy a variety of taste-tempting delights. Best of all, it's an ideal type of dinner party for a small group where each person contributes a dish.❖

Florentine Spread

Cook egg and bacon ahead of time; then you can make it in a flash.

1 (10-oz.) pkg. frozen chopped spinach, thawed, or 1-1/2 cups cooked fresh spinach
1 hard-cooked egg, chopped
4 crisp-cooked bacon slices, crumbled
1 (8-oz.) can water chestnuts, drained, chopped

1/4 cup minced green onions
1/4 teaspoon garlic salt
1/2 teaspoon salt
1 cup plain yogurt
Pimiento
Melba toast or crackers

In a strainer, drain spinach; press with the back of a spoon to remove excess water. In a medium bowl, combine drained spinach, egg, bacon, water chestnuts, green onions, garlic salt and salt. Stir yogurt until smooth; add to spinach mixture. Spoon mixture into a serving dish. Garnish with pimiento. Serve as a spread with Melba toast or crackers. Makes about 3 cups.

Mock-Caviar Spread

Looks and tastes like the real thing.

1 (8-oz.) pkg. cream cheese, room temperature
1/2 cup dairy sour cream
1 (6-oz. net dr. wt.) can pitted ripe olives, drained
1 (2-oz.) can anchovy fillets, drained, chopped

1 tablespoon lemon juice
2 hard-cooked eggs, chopped
1/4 cup finely chopped green onions
Thinly sliced pumpernickel bread or Melba toast

In a small bowl, combine cream cheese and sour cream until smooth. Spread cream-cheese mixture on the bottom of an 8-inch springform pan. Refrigerate while making topping. In a blender or food processor, combine olives, anchovies and lemon juice; process until finely chopped or consistency of caviar. Spread olive mixture over cream-cheese mixture. Top with an outer circle of egg and a center of green onions. Cover and refrigerate at least 2 hours. Remove side of pan. Serve as a spread on pumpernickel bread or Melba toast. Makes 35 to 40 appetizer servings.

Wine-Country Brie

Equally good on an appetizer tray or as a dessert with fresh fruit.

1 (8-oz.) pkg. California Brie cheese
1/2 cup sauterne
1/2 cup butter, room temperature
1/3 cup finely chopped toasted blanched almonds

Crackers
Grapes and sliced pears or apples

Cut cheese in 1/2-inch pieces; place in a small deep bowl. Pour sauterne over cheese. Cover and refrigerate 4 hours or overnight. Drain cheese, discarding sauterne. Cream together cheese and butter until smooth. If too soft to shape in a ball, refrigerate a few minutes. When more firm, shape in a ball. Flatten ball to about 4 inches in diameter, making a *wheel*. Coat entire wheel with almonds. Serve as a spread for crackers or on a tray with grapes, pears or apples. Makes 1 (4-inch) cheese wheel.

Hot Artichoke-Cheese Spread

Water-packed artichokes are preferred for this dish.

1 (8-1/2-oz. net dr. wt.) can artichoke
   hearts, drained, chopped
1 cup dairy sour cream
1 cup grated Parmesan cheese (3 oz.)
1/2 teaspoon garlic salt

1/4 teaspoon seasoned pepper
1/4 cup chopped green onions
1 tablespoon chopped fresh parsley
Crackers or bread sticks

Preheat oven to 350F (175C). In a medium bowl, combine artichoke hearts, sour cream, cheese, garlic salt, seasoned pepper, green onions and parsley. Spoon mixture into a 1-quart baking dish. Bake 12 to 15 minutes or until bubbly. Serve as a spread or dip for crackers or bread sticks. Keep warm on a warming tray or in a chafing dish. Makes about 2-1/2 cups.

Impromptu Shrimp Dip

Put this together in a jiffy when unexpected guests drop in.

1 (4-1/4-oz.) can small shrimp,
   drained, chopped
1/2 cup mayonnaise
1/2 cup dairy sour cream
1 hard-cooked egg, finely chopped
2 green onions, finely chopped

1 teaspoon prepared horseradish
1 tablespoon lemon juice
1 teaspoon Worcestershire sauce
1/2 teaspoon dried dill weed
1/4 teaspoon seasoned salt
Raw vegetable pieces

In a small bowl, combine shrimp, mayonnaise, sour cream, egg, green onions, horseradish, lemon juice, Worcestershire sauce, dill weed and seasoned salt. Spoon into a serving bowl. To serve, place bowl on a tray; surround with raw vegetables such as carrot sticks, cauliflowerets, cherry tomatoes, zucchini sticks and jicama slices. Make dip ahead, if desired. Cover and refrigerate until ready to serve. Makes about 2 cups.

Guacamole

Avocados are picked when firm—be sure to let them ripen at room temperature.

2 large avocados
2 tablespoons lemon juice
1/2 teaspoon salt
2 canned whole green chilies,
   finely chopped
1 teaspoon Worcestershire sauce

1 teaspoon grated onion
3 or 4 drops hot-pepper sauce
1 garlic clove, crushed
1 tomato, chopped, if desired
Corn chips or tortilla chips for dipping

In a small bowl, use a fork to mash avocados. Or, puree avocados in a blender or food processor. Stir in lemon juice, salt, green chilies, Worcestershire sauce, onion, hot-pepper sauce, garlic and tomato, if desired. Serve with corn chips or tortilla chips for dipping. Makes about 1-1/2 cups.

Tip

Puree avocado in a blender or food processor for a smoother dip.

Ribbon Salmon Pâté

An elegant appetizer, perfect to serve for special occasions.

3 hard-cooked eggs, sliced crosswise
3/4 lb. fresh salmon fillets or steaks
1 teaspoon salt
1 cup whipping cream
1 egg
2 tablespoons lemon juice
1 lb. white-fish fillets (sole,
    halibut or cod), cut in cubes
1 egg
1/4 cup dry white wine

1/2 teaspoon salt
1/4 teaspoon pepper
2 tablespoons minced shallots or
    green onion
1 teaspoon dried dill weed
1/2 cup dairy sour cream
Fresh dill for garnish
Lemon slices for garnish
French bread or Melba toast

Line bottom and 1 row along sides of a 9'' x 5'' loaf pan with egg slices. Trim skin, fat and bone from salmon; cut into cubes. In a blender or food processor, combine salmon cubes, 1 teaspoon salt, whipping cream, 1 egg and lemon juice; process until smooth. Spoon salmon mixture evenly on top of egg slices in loaf pan. Lightly press salmon mixture with back of a spoon to remove any air pockets. Preheat oven to 375F (190C). In a blender or food processor, combine white fish, 1 egg, wine, 1/2 teaspoon salt, pepper, shallots or green onion, dill weed and sour cream; process until smooth. Spoon evenly over salmon mixture. Lightly press with back of a spoon to remove any air pockets. Cover with foil. Set loaf pan in á 13'' x 9'' baking pan. Fill larger pan with boiling water to within 1 inch of top. Bake 1 hour or until mixture is firmly set. Remove loaf pan from water. Cool pâté in pan 15 minutes. Loosen sides with a spatula; unmold on a platter. Refrigerate 2 hours or until cool. Garnish with fresh dill and lemon slices. Serve with French bread or Melba toast. Makes 15 to 20 buffet servings or 30 to 40 appetizer servings.

Celebration Caviar Spread

Make the spread ahead; add topping at serving time.

1 cup cottage cheese (8 oz.)
2/3 cup mayonnaise
1 (3-oz.) pkg. cream cheese,
    room temperature
1 tablespoon lemon juice
1 teaspoon prepared mustard
1 teaspoon Worcestershire sauce
1/4 teaspoon seasoned salt

1/4 cup dry white wine
1 (.25-oz.) envelope unflavored gelatin
1 (2-oz.) jar red, golden or black caviar
3 hard-cooked eggs, finely chopped
2 green onions, finely chopped
Thinly sliced pumpernickel bread or
    rye bread

In a blender or food processor, combine cottage cheese, mayonnaise, cream cheese, lemon juice, mustard, Worcestershire sauce and seasoned salt; process until smooth. Pour wine in a small saucepan. Sprinkle gelatin over wine; let stand 5 minutes to soften. Cook over low heat, stirring constantly, until gelatin dissolves. Gradually stir dissolved-gelatin mixture into cottage-cheese mixture. Pour into an 8- or 9-inch quiche pan with a removable bottom or a springform pan. Refrigerate 2 hours or until firm. Remove side of pan. Place spread on a large round platter. Spoon caviar in a 1-inch-wide ring around outer edge on top of spread. Spoon about half the chopped eggs in a 1-1/2-inch-wide ring inside caviar ring. Make a 1/2-inch-wide ring of caviar inside chopped-egg ring. Fill center with remaining chopped eggs. Sprinkle green onions over eggs and caviar. Serve as a spread with pumpernickel or rye bread. Makes 35 to 40 appetizer servings.

Ribbon Salmon Pâté

Cheese-Asparagus Roll-Ups

Serve roll-ups hot from the oven for best flavor.

14 slices sandwich bread
1 (8-oz.) pkg. California Brie cheese,
  room temperature
1 tablespoon whipping cream

1/4 teaspoon fines herbes
14 asparagus spears, cooked, drained
2 tablespoons butter, melted

Preheat broiler. Trim off bread crusts; flatten bread slightly by using light pressure on a rolling pin. In a medium bowl, beat together cheese, cream and fines herbes. Spread about 1 tablespoon cheese mixture on each bread slice. Place 1 asparagus spear on each slice; roll carefully, enclosing asparagus. Place rolls on a broiler pan, seam-side down. Brush with butter. Broil, 6 inches from heat, until golden. Cut each roll in thirds. Serve warm. Makes 42 appetizer servings.

Artichoke-Cheese Wedges

Similar to quiche, but without a crust.

6 eggs
1/3 cup all-purpose flour
3/4 teaspoon baking powder
1/2 teaspoon seasoned salt
1/4 teaspoon seasoned pepper
2 cups shredded sharp Cheddar cheese
  (8 oz.)

1 cup cottage cheese (8 oz.)
1 (8-1/2-oz.) can artichoke hearts,
  drained, chopped
1 tablespoon chopped pimiento
12 to 15 cherry tomatoes,
  cut in halves

Preheat oven to 350F (175C). In a large bowl, beat eggs until thick and lemon-colored, about 5 minutes. Stir in flour, baking powder, seasoned salt and seasoned pepper. Fold in Cheddar cheese, cottage cheese, artichoke hearts and pimiento. Spoon into an 11-inch tart or quiche pan. Bake 25 to 30 minutes or until mixture is firm. Let stand about 10 minutes. To serve, cut in thin wedges. Garnish with cherry-tomato halves. Makes 25 to 30 appetizer servings.

Jalapeño Shrimp

If you don't like it hot, leave out one jalapeño.

1 lb. uncooked medium-large shrimp
  (30 to 40 shrimp)
1 cup white-wine vinegar
1/2 cup vegetable oil
2 fresh jalapeño peppers, seeded,
  cut in matchstick pieces

1 red or green bell pepper, seeded,
  cut in matchstick pieces
2 green onions, minced
1/2 teaspoon seasoned salt

In a medium saucepan, bring 4 to 6 cups water to a boil. Drop shrimp in boiling water. Simmer 2 to 3 minutes or until shrimp become pink; drain, shell and devein shrimp. In a medium bowl, combine shelled shrimp, vinegar, oil, jalapeño peppers, bell pepper, green onions and seasoned salt. Cover and refrigerate 6 hours or overnight. Stir at least once. Serve with wooden picks. Makes 30 to 40 appetizer servings.

How to Make Cheese-Asparagus Roll-Ups

1/Trim off bread crusts; flatten bread slightly, using light pressure on a rolling pin.

2/Place an asparagus spear on each bread slice; roll bread carefully, enclosing asparagus.

Smoked-Oyster-Stuffed Mushrooms

Be sure to use smoked oysters—fresh ones will not give the same results.

1 lb. medium mushrooms, about 40
2 tablespoons butter or margarine
2 tablespoons all-purpose flour
1 cup hot milk
1/8 teaspoon seasoned salt
1/8 teaspoon seasoned pepper

1/2 teaspoon curry powder
1 (3-3/4-oz.) can smoked oysters,
drained, chopped
1 teaspoon lemon juice
Parsley sprigs
Pimiento strips

Preheat oven to 375F (190C). Remove stems from mushrooms; set mushroom caps aside. Finely chop stems; set aside. In a medium saucepan, melt butter or margarine; stir in flour. Cook, stirring over medium heat, about 1 minute. Add hot milk, seasoned salt, seasoned pepper and curry powder. Cook, stirring constantly, 3 minutes or until thickened. Remove from heat; stir in oysters, chopped mushroom stems and lemon juice. Spoon some oyster mixture into each mushroom cap. Place each mushroom, stuffed-side up, in a 13'' x 9'' baking pan. Pour 3/4 cup hot water in bottom of pan, being careful not to pour water on mushrooms. Bake 10 minutes or until mushrooms are hot. Remove baked mushrooms from pan, discarding any remaining liquid. Garnish each stuffed mushroom with a tiny sprig of parsley and a small strip of pimiento. Serve warm. Makes about 40 appetizer servings.

How to Make Tuna-Butter Flutes

1/Use a sharp knife or zucchini cutter and an iced-tea spoon to hollow-out center of French loaf.

2/Spoon refrigerated tuna mixture into both ends of bread until mixture fills loaf.

Stuffed Spiced Kumquats

Kumquats are entirely edible—including the peel.

**18 to 20 fresh unpeeled kumquats
  (about 1/2 lb.)**
1/2 cup white-wine vinegar
1/3 cup honey
1 (4-inch) cinnamon stick
1 teaspoon whole cloves
**1 (3-oz.) pkg. cream cheese,
  room temperature**

1 tablespoon milk
**2 tablespoons finely chopped
  toasted blanched almonds**
**36 to 40 toasted slivered almonds,
  about 2 tablespoons**

Cut each kumquat in half; remove seeds and tough center membrane. In a medium saucepan, combine vinegar, honey, cinnamon stick, cloves and halved kumquats. Bring to a boil; simmer 10 to 12 minutes or until kumquats look translucent. Place waxed paper under 2 cooling racks; drain kumquats, cut-side down, on racks. Discard cooking liquid. In a small bowl, combine cream cheese, milk and chopped almonds. Spoon cheese mixture into each drained kumquat half. Garnish each with a toasted slivered almond. Serve as an appetizer or as a garnish on a cold-meat platter. Makes 36 to 40 appetizer servings.

Tip

To blanch almonds, pour boiling water over shelled whole almonds. Let stand 1 minute or until skins are loose. Drain and cover with cold water. Pinch or rub off skins with your fingertips.

Tuna-Butter Flutes

In a French bakery, this narrow loaf of bread is known as a baguette.

1 (6-oz.) loaf French bread,
  about 11" x 2"
1 (9-1/4-oz.) can oil- or water-pack
  tuna, drained

1/2 cup unsalted butter, melted
1 tablespoon chopped fresh parsley
1 tablespoon lemon juice
Parsley sprigs, if desired

Cut a 1/2-inch slice off each end of bread. Working from both ends, use a sharp narrow knife or a zucchini cutter and an iced-tea spoon to hollow-out center of loaf. Leave about a 1/4-inch shell of bread. In a blender or food processor, combine tuna, butter, parsley and lemon juice; process until smooth. Refrigerate until tuna mixture nearly holds its shape. Spoon tuna mixture into both ends of bread until it meets in center. Wrap loaf in foil or plastic wrap. Refrigerate 2 hours or until cold and filling is firm. Using a sharp knife, cut 3/8-inch-thick crosswise slices. Garnish with parsley sprigs, if desired. Makes about 30 appetizer servings.

Gazpacho Blanco

Use white or light-green vegetables to keep the mixture light-colored.

2 cucumbers, peeled
2 green onions, white and
  light-green parts chopped
2 light-green celery stalks, diced
2 tablespoons white-wine vinegar
1/2 teaspoon salt

1/4 teaspoon white pepper
1 garlic clove, crushed
1 cup dairy sour cream
1 cup plain yogurt
2 cups chicken stock or bouillon
Chopped green-onion tops

Cut each cucumber in half lengthwise; scoop out and discard seeds. Dice cucumber halves. In a blender or food processor, puree diced cucumbers, green onions, celery, vinegar, salt, pepper and garlic. In a large bowl, combine sour cream and yogurt. Stir in pureed-cucumber mixture and stock or bouillon. Chill until ready to serve. Pour soup in a tureen or individual soup bowls. Garnish with green-onion tops. Makes 6 appetizer servings.

Summertime Avocado Soup

A cool refreshing first course for hot-weather entertaining.

2 avocados, diced
1/2 cup dairy sour cream
2 tablespoons chopped green onion
2 tablespoons canned diced green chilies,
  drained

1 tablespoon lemon juice
1/2 teaspoon seasoned salt
1/4 teaspoon garlic salt
2 cups chicken stock or bouillon
1 tomato, finely chopped

In a blender or food processor, puree avocados, sour cream, green onion, green chilies and lemon juice. In a medium bowl, combine avocado puree, seasoned salt, garlic salt and stock or bouillon. Chill until ready to serve. Pour soup in a tureen or individual soup bowls. Sprinkle tomato over top. Makes 4 to 5 appetizer servings.

Ways with California Nuts

Here are six snack ideas featuring California nuts. You may want to substitute additional kinds of your favorite nuts.

Honeyed Pine Nuts

1/4 cup butter or margarine, melted
2 tablespoons honey

1/4 teaspoon grated orange peel
1 cup shelled pine nuts or slivered almonds

Preheat oven to 300F (150C). In a medium bowl, combine butter or margarine, honey and orange peel. Stir in nuts. Spread nut mixture in a shallow baking pan. Bake 15 minutes, stirring at least once during baking time. Makes 1 cup.

Deviled Sunflower Nuts

2 tablespoons butter or margarine
1 cup sunflower nuts
1/2 teaspoon prepared mustard
1/2 teaspoon Worcestershire sauce

1/8 teaspoon paprika
1/4 teaspoon salt
Dash of hot-pepper sauce

In a medium skillet, melt butter or margarine. Add sunflower nuts. Cook, stirring, over low heat 5 minutes. Stir in mustard, Worcestershire sauce, paprika, salt and hot-pepper sauce. Cook, stirring, 1 minute. Makes 1 cup.

Glazed Pistachios

2 tablespoons butter or margarine
1/2 cup sugar

Dash of ground cinnamon
1 cup shelled pistachios

In a large skillet, melt butter or margarine. Stir in sugar, cinnamon and pistachios. Cook over medium heat, stirring constantly, until sugar turns to a golden liquid. Drop mixture by teaspoonfuls on a piece of foil. Makes about 25 clusters.

Spiced Walnuts

2 tablespoons sugar
1 teaspoon ground cinnamon
1/4 teaspoon ground allspice

1/4 teaspoon ground mace
1/4 cup butter or margarine, melted
2 cups walnut halves or pieces

Preheat oven to 325F (165C). In a medium bowl, combine sugar, cinnamon, allspice and mace; stir in butter or margarine. Add walnuts; toss to coat. Spread in a single layer on a shallow baking pan. Bake 10 minutes, stirring once during baking time. Makes about 2 cups.

Garlic-Cheese Almonds

1 tablespoon butter or margarine, melted
1 tablespoon vegetable oil
1 cup whole unblanched almonds

1/4 cup grated Parmesan cheese (3/4 oz.)
1/2 teaspoon garlic salt

Preheat oven to 400F (205C). In a small bowl, combine butter or margarine and oil. Pour almonds into butter mixture; toss to coat. Using a slotted spoon, remove almonds; place in a shallow baking pan. Bake 5 minutes. In a small bowl, combine cheese and garlic salt. Upon removing almonds from oven, drop them into cheese mixture. Toss to thoroughly coat almonds. Makes about 1 cup.

Salads & Dressings

S alads are one of California's most famous products. Dozens of products are available year round for making interesting combinations.

GREENS

The basis of most salads is usually greens. Whether it's a few lettuce leaves under a gelatin salad or greens in a tossed salad, the ingredients should be fresh and crisp.

Popular greens include iceberg, romaine, Boston and leaf lettuce. Lend variety to your salads with one or more of the lesser known greens. Try the pale-green leaves of Chinese or Napa cabbage. Savoy cabbage, with its thick sturdy leaves, makes an impressive lining for a salad bowl. Arugula, a leaf with slightly bitter flavor, and radicchio, a red leaf, are two European newcomers. Both are popular with some California restaurants. Watercress, cilantro, alfalfa sprouts and chives contribute new flavors to salads.

OILS & FLAVORED VINEGARS

Cider vinegar is generally used for salad dressings, pickles and relishes. Both white-wine vinegar and red-wine vinegar make good bases for salad dressings. Gourmet specialty stores have other flavored vinegars. If you enjoy fresh herbs or spices, you can easily make your own specialty vinegars. Place desired herb in a bottle. Fill bottle with cider vinegar or wine vinegar. If you want a slight hint of herb, dilute the full-strength flavored vinegar by adding an equal amount of cider vinegar or wine vinegar.

Oils from peanuts, corn and soybeans are light and mild in flavor. They're popular for vinaigrette dressings and homemade mayonnaise. Walnut and sesame oils are fairly strong and should be diluted with one of the milder varieties.

FRUIT FOR SALADS

Take advantage of fresh fruits in season when most reasonably priced. Remember that fruits like bananas, oranges and apples, are always with us. Fruit salads are colorful, so think of combinations that taste good and present a showy appearance.

MAIN-DISH SALADS

Main-dish salads can be a combination of fruits or vegetables teamed with meat, fish, cheese or poultry. The traditional Cobb Salad originated at the Brown Derby restaurant in Hollywood. It's a hearty salad that combines bacon, chicken and eggs with greens.❖

Smoked-Turkey Salad

Purchase smoked turkey at a deli or smoke your own, page 103.

1 cup slivered smoked turkey or chicken
1 cup white seedless or seeded Tokay grapes,
   cut in halves
2 cups shredded lettuce (1/2 small head)
2 oz. California goat cheese,
   cut in 1/2-inch cubes

1/3 cup walnut oil or vegetable oil
3 tablespoons dry red wine
1/4 teaspoon dry mustard
1/4 teaspoon salt
1/8 teaspoon pepper
Pomegranate seeds

In a large bowl, combine turkey or chicken, grapes, lettuce and cheese. In a small bowl, combine oil, wine, mustard, salt and pepper. Pour oil mixture over turkey or chicken mixture; toss lightly. To serve, spoon salad on 4 or 5 individual salad plates. Sprinkle pomegranate seeds over each salad. Makes 4 to 5 servings.

Mustardy Ham Salad

A main-dish salad with a kick to it.

8 oz. cooked ham
1 small head lettuce, broken in chunks
4 hard-cooked eggs, sliced
3 tomatoes, cut in wedges
1 cup cooked green peas or green beans,
   chilled
3 green onions, sliced

1/2 cup dairy sour cream
1/4 cup Dijon-style mustard
2 tablespoons sugar
1/8 teaspoon salt
2 tablespoons white-wine vinegar
1 teaspoon dried dill weed
1/4 cup vegetable oil

Cut ham in strips about 1/4 inch thick and 1/2 inch wide. Line a large salad bowl or 6 individual salad bowls with lettuce. Arrange ham strips, eggs, tomatoes and peas or green beans on lettuce. Sprinkle green onions over salad. In a small bowl, combine sour cream and mustard; add sugar, salt, vinegar and dill weed. Gradually pour in oil, stirring constantly. Spoon over salad. Serve immediately. Makes 6 servings.

Imperial Luncheon Plate

Impressive fare for those VIPs in your life.

1/3 cup dairy sour cream
1/3 cup mayonnaise
2 teaspoons white-wine vinegar
1/2 teaspoon dried leaf tarragon, crumbled
1/4 teaspoon dried leaf basil, crumbled
2 teaspoons Dijon-style mustard
1 tablespoon minced green onion

1/2 teaspoon prepared horseradish
4 cups shredded lettuce
2 cups shredded cooked crabmeat
   (about 12 oz.)
2 hard-cooked eggs, cut in quarters
4 artichoke hearts, cooked, cooled
12 asparagus spears, cooked, cooled

In a medium bowl, combine sour cream, mayonnaise, vinegar, tarragon, basil, mustard, green onion and horseradish; set aside. Line 4 luncheon plates with lettuce. Sprinkle 1/2 cup crabmeat over each lettuce-lined plate. On each plate, arrange 2 quarters of hard-cooked egg, 1 artichoke heart and 3 asparagus spears. Spoon sour-cream mixture over each salad. Serve immediately. Makes 4 servings.

Shredded-Beef Salad

A hearty and satisfying salad.

1 (2-1/2- to 3-lb.) beef chuck
   7-bone pot roast
1 (16-oz.) can tomatoes, cut-up
1 garlic clove, minced
1 teaspoon chili powder
1 teaspoon salt

1 small bunch leaf lettuce, chopped
1 (15-oz.) can pinto beans, drained
4 oz. Monterey Jack cheese,
   cut in small strips
1 avocado, chopped
1 cup Italian salad dressing

Place beef roast in a large pan; add tomatoes, garlic, chili powder and salt. Cover and simmer 2 to 3 hours or until beef is very tender. Cool beef and tomato mixture. Remove beef from tomato mixture; discard tomato mixture. Remove and discard beef bones. Using 2 forks, pull beef into shreds. In a large salad bowl, combine shredded beef, lettuce, beans, cheese and avocado. Pour Italian dressing over salad; toss lightly. Serve immediately. Makes 6 main-dish servings.

Mariachi Salad

For a festive presentation, serve in a crisp-fried flour tortilla.

2 avocados
1/4 cup canned diced green chilies, drained
1 garlic clove, minced
3 tablespoons lemon juice
1/2 cup dairy sour cream
1/2 teaspoon salt
1 small head lettuce

2 tomatoes, cut in 1/2-inch chunks
3 green onions, sliced
1 cup pitted ripe olives, cut in halves
1 cup diced sharp or mild Cheddar cheese
   (4 oz.)
1 cup corn chips, crushed

In a medium bowl, use a fork to mash avocados. Stir in green chilies, garlic, lemon juice, sour cream and salt. Cover and refrigerate 1 hour. To serve, tear lettuce in bite-size pieces; place in a large salad bowl. Add tomatoes, green onions, olives and cheese. Spoon avocado mixture over salad; toss lightly. Sprinkle corn chips over salad. Serve immediately. Makes 6 to 8 servings.

Tarragon-Chicken Platter

Makes a superb summer luncheon served with crusty French rolls and iced tea.

1/2 cup mayonnaise
1/4 cup plain yogurt
1 tablespoon lemon juice
1/4 teaspoon Dijon-style mustard
1 tablespoon chopped fresh parsley
1 teaspoon dried leaf tarragon, crumbled

1/2 teaspoon salt
1/8 teaspoon pepper
3 cups diced cooked chicken
Lettuce leaves
2 tomatoes, cut in quarters
1 cucumber, cut in 8 sticks

In a medium bowl, combine mayonnaise, yogurt, lemon juice, mustard, parsley, tarragon, salt and pepper; stir in chicken. Cover and refrigerate 2 to 3 hours for flavors to blend. To serve, arrange lettuce leaves on 4 individual salad plates. Spoon chicken mixture on each lettuce-lined plate. Garnish each salad with tomatoes and cucumbers. Makes 4 servings.

Summertime Chicken Salad

A perfect main-dish salad for hot-weather luncheons.

1/2 cup dairy sour cream
1/2 cup mayonnaise
2 teaspoons minced crystallized ginger
2 tablespoons chutney, fruit pieces and
   juice
1/4 teaspoon curry powder

4 cups diced cooked chicken
1 cup seedless grapes
1 cup fresh pineapple chunks
2 small cantaloupe or honeydew melons
Lettuce leaves
1/4 cup toasted slivered almonds

In a small bowl, combine sour cream, mayonnaise, ginger, chutney and curry powder. In a medium bowl, combine chicken, grapes and pineapple. Pour sour-cream mixture over chicken mixture; toss lightly. Peel melons. Cut each melon in 3 thick crosswise slices. Remove and discard seeds. Line 6 individual salad plates with lettuce. Arrange 1 melon slice on each plate. Spoon chicken mixture into center of each melon slice. To serve, sprinkle almonds over each serving. Makes 6 servings.

Golden State Salad

Practically a complete meal in one dish.

6 oz. fresh or frozen pea pods
1 small head cauliflower
2 carrots, cut in matchstick pieces
1 (8-oz.) can water chestnuts,
   drained, sliced
2 green onions, thinly sliced
1 cup alfalfa sprouts

2 cup cooked chicken,
   cut in bite-size pieces
1/4 cup vegetable oil
2 tablespoons white-wine vinegar
2 tablespoons soy sauce
1/4 teaspoon garlic salt
2 tablespoons toasted sesame seeds

Place pea pods in a medium, heatproof bowl. To cook pea pods, pour 2 cups boiling water over pods. Let stand 1 minute; drain and cool. Break cauliflower in flowerets; cut flowerets in thin slices. In a large salad bowl, combine cooked pea pods, cauliflower, carrots, water chestnuts, green onions, alfalfa sprouts and chicken. In a small bowl, combine oil, vinegar, soy sauce and garlic salt. Pour over pea-pod mixture; toss lightly. To serve, sprinkle with sesame seeds. Makes 4 to 6 servings.

Overnight Trade-Winds Salad

A wonderful make-ahead salad for a summer buffet.

1 cup uncooked white rice
3 cups diced cooked chicken or turkey
1 cup chopped celery
1 (8-oz.) can crushed pineapple, drained
1/4 cup flaked coconut

1 cup mayonnaise
2 tablespoons white-wine vinegar
1/2 teaspoon salt
2 teaspoons curry powder
1/2 cup chopped cashews

Cook rice according to package directions; cool. In a large salad bowl, combine cooked rice, chicken or turkey, celery, pineapple and coconut. In a small bowl, combine mayonnaise, vinegar, salt and curry powder. Pour mayonnaise mixture over rice mixture; toss lightly. Cover and refrigerate several hours or overnight. To serve, sprinkle cashews over salad. Makes 6 to 8 servings.

Summertime Chicken Salad, above; Springtime Asparagus Salad, page 31; Broccoli-Bacon Salad, page 42; and Herb Vinegars, page 44.

Marinated-Vegetable Medley

Almost a meal in itself; crisp and refreshing.

1/2 cup vegetable oil
1/4 cup lemon juice
1 garlic clove, crushed
1/2 teaspoon salt
1/8 teaspoon pepper
1/2 teaspoon dried leaf basil, crushed
1/2 lb. fresh broccoli
   (about 1 large stalk)
2 carrots, sliced diagonally

1 celery stalk, thinly sliced crosswise
1 small onion, thinly sliced
1/4 lb. small whole mushrooms
   (if medium or large in size,
   slice or cut in halves)
1 zucchini, sliced
8 cherry tomatoes, cut in halves
Lettuce leaves

In a small bowl, combine oil, lemon juice, garlic, salt, pepper and basil; set aside. Cut broccoli in flowerets; thinly slice broccoli stalk diagonally. In a large bowl, combine broccoli, carrots, celery, onion, mushrooms and zucchini. Add oil mixture; toss lightly. Cover and refrigerate several hours or overnight, stirring occasionally. To serve, gently stir in tomatoes. Line a large salad bowl with lettuce leaves. Spoon marinated vegetables into lettuce-lined bowl. Makes 5 to 6 servings.

Harvest Salad

A dramatic color and flavor combination.

Romaine lettuce or curly endive
2 grapefruit, seeded, sectioned
2 avocados, sliced
2 persimmons, sliced
1/3 cup vegetable oil

3 tablespoons red-wine vinegar
1/4 teaspoon salt
1 teaspoon honey
1/2 teaspoon Dijon-style mustard
2 tablespoons pomegranate seeds

Cover a large plate with romaine or endive leaves. Top with an arrangement of alternating grapefruit sections, avocado slices and persimmon slices. In a small bowl, combine oil, vinegar, salt, honey and mustard; drizzle oil mixture over fruit. Sprinkle salad with pomegranate seeds. Serve immediately. Makes 6 to 8 servings.

Prize-Winning Macaroni Salad   *Photo on page 107.*

Most popular candidate for picnics and potluck dinners.

8 oz. uncooked small elbow macaroni
1 cup mayonnaise
2 tablespoons vinegar
1 teaspoon sugar
2 teaspoons prepared mustard
1/4 teaspoon celery seed
1 teaspoon salt

1/8 teaspoon pepper
1 cup diced Cheddar cheese (4 oz.)
1 cup cooked green peas
1/2 cup diced celery
1/4 cup minced onion
1/4 cup chopped sweet pickle

Cook macaroni according to package directions; drain. Pour cold water over macaroni; let stand while preparing salad. In a small bowl, combine mayonnaise, vinegar, sugar, mustard, celery seed, salt and pepper. Drain cooked macaroni. In a large salad bowl, combine cooked macaroni, cheese, peas, celery, onion and pickle. Pour mayonnaise mixture over macaroni mixture; toss to blend. Serve immediately, or cover and refrigerate until ready to serve. Makes 6 to 8 servings.

Springtime Asparagus Salad   *Photo on page 28.*

A light refreshing salad—ideal with hearty entrees.

2 lbs. fresh asparagus spears
3/4 cup vegetable oil
1/3 cup Tarragon Vinegar, page 44
1 tablespoon chopped green onion
1 tablespoon chopped pimiento
1 tablespoon chopped fresh parsley

2 tablespoons sweet pickle relish
1/2 teaspoon salt
1/4 teaspoon pepper
Boston or Bibb lettuce, if desired
2 hard-cooked eggs, chopped

Break off and discard about 2 inches of the tough end of each asparagus spear. In a medium saucepan, steam or boil asparagus spears 12 to 15 minutes or until tender; drain and cool. In a small bowl, combine oil, vinegar, green onion, pimiento, parsley, relish, salt and pepper. Place cooked asparagus spears in a shallow bowl; pour oil mixture over asparagus. Cover and refrigerate at least 2 hours or overnight. To serve, drain asparagus. Arrange lettuce leaves in a salad bowl or on 6 to 8 individual salad plates, if desired. Arrange spears on lettuce leaves. Sprinkle egg over asparagus. Makes 6 to 8 servings.

Classic Caesar Salad

A popular salad which originated on the West Coast.

1 garlic clove, crushed
1/3 cup olive oil or vegetable oil
1 cup sourdough bread cubes
   (about 1/2-inch)
1 egg
1/4 teaspoon salt

1/8 teaspoon pepper
1/8 teaspoon Worcestershire sauce
2 or 3 anchovy fillets, if desired
1 head romaine lettuce
2 tablespoons lemon juice
1/4 cup grated Parmesan cheese (3/4 oz.)

In a measuring cup, combine garlic and oil several hours ahead, if possible. Drizzle about 1 tablespoon garlic-seasoned oil over bread cubes. In a small skillet, brown bread cubes over low heat or in a 300F (150C) oven 20 minutes or until crisp; set aside to cool. In a small saucepan, bring a small amount of water to a boil. Gently place egg in boiling water; let stand 1 minute. Immediately pour cold water over egg; set aside. In bottom of a large salad bowl, combine half the remaining garlic-seasoned oil, salt, pepper, Worcestershire sauce and anchovies, if desired. Using a fork, mash anchovies into oil mixture. Break romaine lettuce in bite-size pieces; add to oil mixture. Pour remaining garlic-seasoned oil over romaine; toss lightly. Break egg into bowl. Toss to coat leaves. Add lemon juice; toss again. Sprinkle Parmesan cheese over salad; toss again. Top with browned bread cubes. Serve immediately. Makes 5 to 6 servings.

Variation

Short-Cut Caesar Dressing: In a blender or food processor, combine 1/2 cup vegetable oil, 1/4 cup lemon juice, 1 egg, 4 anchovy fillets, 1/8 teaspoon pepper, 1/2 teaspoon prepared mustard and 1 crushed garlic clove. Process until smooth. Add 1-1/4 teaspoons Worcestershire sauce and 1/4 cup grated Parmesan cheese. Refrigerate in a covered container. Makes 1-1/4 cups.

West Coast Salad

Be sure to remove any seeds from tangerine segments.

1 (1-lb.) bunch fresh spinach
1/4 lb. fresh mushrooms, sliced
2 tangerines, separated in segments
1 avocado, sliced
1/3 cup vegetable oil
3 tablespoons red-wine vinegar

1 teaspoon honey
1/4 teaspoon celery salt
1/2 teaspoon salt
1/8 teaspoon pepper
1/4 teaspoon paprika
4 crisp-cooked bacon slices, crumbled

Wash and trim spinach; tear in bite-size pieces. In a large salad bowl, combine spinach, mushrooms, tangerines and avocado. In a small bowl, combine oil, vinegar, honey, celery salt, salt, pepper and paprika. Pour oil mixture over spinach mixture; toss lightly. To serve, sprinkle bacon over salad. Makes 6 servings.

Crunchy Broccoli Salad

Imagine this at your next buffet supper.

2 lbs. fresh broccoli
1/2 cup mayonnaise
1/2 cup dairy sour cream
1 teaspoon sugar
1/4 teaspoon salt
1/8 teaspoon pepper

1 teaspoon grated onion
1 garlic clove, crushed
1 (8-oz.) can water chestnuts,
  drained, sliced
2 tablespoons toasted sesame seeds

Cut off and discard tough ends from broccoli stalks. Cut stalks in 1/2-inch-thick diagonal slices. Break broccoli flowerets in small clusters. Cook broccoli in boiling salted water 10 minutes or until crisp-tender; drain and cool. In a small bowl, combine mayonnaise, sour cream, sugar, salt, pepper, onion and garlic. In a large salad bowl, combine cooked broccoli and water chestnuts. Add mayonnaise mixture; toss lightly. Cover and refrigerate 2 hours or more for flavors to blend. To serve, sprinkle sesame seeds over salad. Makes 5 to 6 servings.

Celery-Root Salad

Celery root, also known as celeriac, is a favorite vegetable in Europe; it's becoming popular in California.

1 lb. celery root
1/4 cup lemon juice
1 teaspoon salt
1/8 teaspoon pepper
1/2 cup dairy sour cream

2 tablespoons minced fresh parsley
1 tablespoon Dijon-style mustard
1/2 teaspoon fines herbes
Lettuce leaves

Peel celery root; shred in a food processor or on the coarse blade of a hand shredder. Place shredded celery root in a large bowl; sprinkle lemon juice, salt and pepper over celery root. In a small bowl, combine sour cream, parsley, mustard and fines herbes. Pour sour-cream mixture over celery-root mixture; toss lightly. To serve, arrange lettuce leaves on 6 to 8 individual salad plates. Spoon celery-root mixture on each lettuce-lined plate. Makes 6 to 8 servings.

Palace Court Salad

Our version of a famous salad originated at the Palace Hotel in San Francisco.

1/2 cup mayonnaise	4 cups shredded lettuce (1 small head)
1/4 cup dairy sour cream	2 large tomatoes
1/4 cup chili sauce	6 large or 18 small cooked artichoke bottoms
2 tablespoons minced fresh parsley	1 lb. cooked small shrimp or flaked crabmeat
1 tablespoon minced shallots or green onion	18 asparagus spears, cooked, cooled
1/2 teaspoon dried leaf tarragon	2 hard-cooked eggs
1/4 teaspoon salt	

In a small bowl, combine mayonnaise, sour cream, chili sauce, parsley, shallots or green onion, tarragon and salt; set aside. Arrange lettuce on 6 individual salad plates. Cut each tomato in 3 thick slices; place 1 slice on each lettuce-lined plate. Arrange 1 large or 3 small artichoke bottoms on each tomato slice. Fill artichoke bottoms with equal portions of shrimp or crabmeat. Arrange 3 asparagus spears on lettuce beside each tomato slice. Spoon mayonnaise mixture over each salad. Sieve hard-cooked egg over each salad. Serve immediately. Makes 6 servings.

Fresh-Mushroom Salad

Slice mushrooms as thin as possible — either by hand or in a food processor.

3 tablespoons Tarragon Vinegar, page 44	1/2 teaspoon salt
1 tablespoon lemon juice	1/4 teaspoon pepper
1/3 cup olive oil or vegetable oil	1 teaspoon Dijon-style mustard
1 tablespoon minced fresh chives	1/4 teaspoon dried leaf chervil, crushed
2 tablespoons minced watercress	1/2 lb. fresh mushrooms, thinly sliced
1 tablespoon minced pimiento	Lettuce leaves

In a small bowl, combine vinegar, lemon juice, oil, chives, watercress, pimiento, salt, pepper, mustard and chervil. Place mushrooms in a medium bowl. Pour vinegar mixture over mushrooms; toss lightly. Line a salad bowl with lettuce leaves. Spoon mushroom mixture into lettuce-lined bowl. Serve immediately. Makes 3 to 4 servings.

Baked Chèvre-Topped Greens

Combine your choice of curly endive, romaine lettuce, radicchio or Boston lettuce.

5 oz. California goat cheese	1/4 teaspoon Dijon-style mustard
1/3 cup fine dry breadcrumbs	1/4 teaspoon salt
1/2 teaspoon fines herbes	1/8 teaspoon pepper
6 tablespoons olive oil	Mixed salad greens
2 tablespoons red-wine vinegar	

Preheat oven to 400F (205C). Lightly grease a small baking pan. Cut cheese in 8 wedges. In a pie plate, combine breadcrumbs and fines herbes. Pour 2 tablespoons oil in a shallow bowl. Dip each cheese wedge in olive oil and then in breadcrumb mixture. Place crumb-coated cheese wedges in greased baking pan. Bake 5 to 7 minutes or until crumbs become golden. While cheese is baking, combine remaining 1/4 cup oil, vinegar, mustard, salt and pepper. In a medium bowl, lightly toss greens with oil mixture. Place seasoned greens on 4 individual salad plates. Top each serving with 2 wedges of hot cheese. Serve immediately. Makes 4 servings.

How to Make Palace Court Salad

1/Place 1 large or 3 small artichoke bottoms on each tomato slice.

2/Press hard-cooked egg through a fine sieve over each salad.

Cobb Salad

Secret of the famous Brown Derby Restaurant salad is finely chopped ingredients.

**6 cups finely shredded lettuce
  (1 medium head)**
**2 cups finely chopped cooked chicken or
  turkey**
6 crisp-cooked bacon slices, crumbled
3 hard-cooked eggs, finely chopped
2 tomatoes, finely chopped
1 avocado, finely chopped
3 green onions, finely chopped
1 bunch watercress, finely chopped
**1/2 cup shredded sharp Cheddar cheese
  (2 oz.)**

2/3 cup vegetable oil
1/2 cup red-wine vinegar
2 tablespoons Worcestershire sauce
1 garlic clove, crushed
1/2 teaspoon dry mustard
1 teaspoon salt
1/4 teaspoon pepper
**1/2 cup crumbled Roquefort or
  blue cheese (2 oz.)**

In a large salad bowl, combine lettuce, chicken or turkey, bacon, eggs, tomatoes, avocado, green onions, watercress and Cheddar cheese. In a small bowl, combine oil, vinegar, Worcestershire sauce, garlic, mustard, salt and pepper. Pour oil mixture over lettuce mixture; toss lightly. Sprinkle Roquefort or blue cheese over salad. Serve immediately. Makes 4 to 5 main-dish servings.

Shown on the following pages: Old Mission Salad

Old Mission Salad   *Photo on pages 36 & 37.*

Colorful salad for a buffet supper.

Bibb or Boston lettuce
3 oranges, peeled, sliced crosswise
1 small red onion, thinly sliced
1 large avocado
2 tablespoons lemon juice
1/4 cup vegetable oil

1/2 teaspoon sugar
1/2 teaspoon salt
1 garlic clove
1/2 teaspoon dry mustard
1/2 cup whole pitted ripe olives

Arrange lettuce leaves on a platter. Top with slices of orange and onion. Cut avocado in 8 to 10 pieces. In a blender or food processor, puree avocado, lemon juice, oil, sugar, salt, garlic and mustard. Spoon avocado mixture over salad. Garnish with ripe olives. Makes 6 servings.

Bahia Cole Slaw

A tropical delight for your next potluck or barbecue.

4 cups shredded cabbage (1 small head)
1/2 cup chopped dates
1 (8-oz.) can crushed pineapple, drained
1/2 cup dairy sour cream
1 tablespoon honey

1 teaspoon lime juice
1 teaspoon finely chopped
  crystallized ginger
1/4 cup flaked coconut

In a large salad bowl, combine cabbage, dates and pineapple. In a small bowl, combine sour cream, honey, lime juice and ginger. Pour sour-cream mixture over cabbage mixture; toss lightly. To serve, sprinkle coconut over salad. Makes 6 servings.

Oriental Cole Slaw

If sesame oil is not available, use vegetable oil.

1 head Chinese or Napa cabbage
1 bunch radishes, thinly sliced
2 cups fresh bean sprouts (about 1/2 lb.)
1 (8-oz.) can water chestnuts,
  drained, sliced
2 green onions, thinly sliced
1/4 cup vegetable oil

2 tablespoons sesame oil
1/3 cup white-wine vinegar
2 tablespoons soy sauce
1/2 teaspoon ground ginger
1/8 teaspoon salt
1 garlic clove, crushed
1/2 teaspoon dry mustard

Remove 5 or 6 outer cabbage leaves; line a large salad bowl with removed leaves. In a second large bowl, shred remaining cabbage; add radishes, bean sprouts, water chestnuts and green onions. In a small bowl, combine vegetable oil, sesame oil, vinegar, soy sauce, ginger, salt, garlic and dry mustard. Pour oil mixture over cabbage mixture; toss lightly. Spoon salad into cabbage-lined bowl. Makes 8 servings.

Tip

When a recipe calls for shredded cabbage, use the coarse side of a hand grater, the shredder blade of your food processor or thinly slice and chop cabbage with a sharp knife.

Rangoon Salad

Pea pods give crisp texture and bright-green color to this salad.

1 cup fresh or frozen pea pods
1 head Boston lettuce,
   torn in bite-size pieces
1 (8-oz.) can water chestnuts,
   drained, sliced
1/3 cup vegetable oil

3 tablespoons red-wine vinegar
2 tablespoons chutney, fruit pieces and
   juice
1 tablespoon prepared mustard
1 garlic clove, crushed
2 crisp-cooked bacon slices, crumbled

Place pea pods in a medium, heatproof bowl. To cook pea pods, pour 2 cups boiling water over pods. Let stand 1 minute; drain and cool. In a large salad bowl, combine lettuce, water chestnuts and cooked pea pods; cover and refrigerate. In a blender or food processor, combine oil, vinegar, chutney, mustard and garlic; process until smooth. Pour oil mixture over salad; toss lightly. To serve, sprinkle bacon over salad. Makes 5 to 6 servings.

High-Noon Fruit Salad

Serve with popovers or Triple-Wheat Muffins, page 57.

1/4 cup mayonnaise
1/4 cup dairy sour cream
2 tablespoons orange juice
1/2 teaspoon grated orange peel
1/8 teaspoon paprika
1 tablespoon honey

1/3 cup finely chopped toasted almonds
Lettuce leaves
2 bananas, cut in chunks
2 cups fresh blueberries
2 cups honeydew-melon balls
2 peaches, peeled, sliced

In a small bowl, combine mayonnaise and sour cream. Stir in orange juice, orange peel, paprika, honey and almonds. Arrange lettuce leaves on a large shallow platter or 6 individual luncheon plates. Arrange bananas, blueberries, melon and peaches on lettuce-lined platter or plates. Spoon mayonnaise mixture over fruit. Serve immediately. Makes 6 servings.

Fruit & Cheese Salad

For best flavor, chill two hours or longer.

2 oranges, diced
1 cup seeded Tokay-grape halves
2 pears, peeled, diced
8 oz. Swiss cheese, diced
2 tablespoons crumbled blue cheese
   (about 1 oz.)

1/2 cup mayonnaise
1/2 teaspoon prepared mustard
1 tablespoon white-wine vinegar
1/2 teaspoon sugar
1/8 teaspoon garlic salt
Lettuce leaves

In a large bowl, combine oranges, grapes, pears and Swiss cheese. In a small bowl, combine blue cheese and mayonnaise; stir in mustard, vinegar, sugar and garlic salt. Add blue-cheese mixture to fruit and cheese; toss lightly. Cover and refrigerate. To serve, line a large salad bowl with lettuce leaves. Spoon chilled salad into lettuce-lined bowl. Serve immediately. Makes 6 to 8 servings.

Turkey & Cranberry Layered Salad

Enjoy a tasty salad made from Thanksgiving leftovers.

Turkey Layer:
1/4 cup cold water
1 (.25-oz.) envelope unflavored gelatin
1 cup mayonnaise
1/2 cup dairy sour cream

2 cups chopped cooked turkey or chicken
1/4 cup finely chopped celery
1 tablespoon finely chopped green onion
1/2 teaspoon salt

Cranberry Layer:
1/4 cup cold water
1 (.25-oz.) envelope unflavored gelatin
1 cup orange juice
1 (8-oz.) can whole-cranberry sauce (1 cup)
1/4 cup slivered almonds

Dash ground cloves
Lettuce leaves
Celery leaves
Orange slices

Turkey Layer:
Pour water in a small saucepan. Sprinkle gelatin over cold water; let stand 5 minutes to soften. Cook over low heat, stirring constantly, until gelatin dissolves; remove from heat. In a medium bowl, gradually stir warm gelatin mixture into mayonnaise. Add sour cream, turkey or chicken, celery, green onion and salt. Pour gelatin mixture into a 6-cup mold. Refrigerate until nearly firm, but sticky on top.

Cranberry Layer:
Pour water in a small saucepan. Sprinkle gelatin over cold water; let stand 5 minutes to soften. Add orange juice. Cook mixture over low heat, stirring constantly, until gelatin dissolves; remove from heat. Add cranberry sauce, almonds and cloves; let stand at room temperature until turkey layer is nearly firm. Carefully spoon cranberry mixture over turkey layer. Refrigerate until firm. To serve, line a plate with lettuce leaves. Unmold salad onto lettuce-lined plate. Garnish with celery leaves and orange slices. Makes 6 to 8 servings.

Emerald Cove Mold

Avocados are a good source of vitamin A and potassium.

1 cup Green-Goddess Dressing, page 42
2 cups chicken stock or bouillon
2 (.25-oz.) envelopes unflavored gelatin
2 avocados
2 tablespoons lemon juice

2 tablespoons canned diced green chilies, drained
2 green onions, chopped
1 tomato, chopped

Prepare Green-Goddess Dressing. Pour stock or bouillon in a small saucepan. Sprinkle gelatin over stock or bouillon; let stand 5 minutes to soften. Cook over low heat, stirring constantly, until gelatin dissolves; remove from heat. Stir in Green-Goddess Dressing. Slice avocados. In a blender or food processor, puree avocados, lemon juice, 1 cup gelatin mixture, green chilies and green onions. Stir pureed avocado mixture into remaining gelatin mixture; refrigerate until syrupy. Stir and pour partially set gelatin mixture into a 1-1/2-quart bowl. Refrigerate 4 hours or until firm. To serve, garnish top with a ring of chopped tomato. Makes 6 servings.

How to Make Turkey & Cranberry Layered Salad

1/Pour cranberry mixture over chilled turkey layer.

2/Garnish salad with celery leaves and orange slices.

Mandarin-Chicken Platter

A great make-ahead brunch pleaser.

1 (12-oz.) can apricot nectar
2 (.25-oz.) envelopes unflavored gelatin
2 cups orange juice
1/2 cup chutney, fruit pieces and juice
2 cups diced cooked chicken
1 tangerine, sectioned, seeded

1 banana, diced
1/4 cup chopped peanuts
1/2 cup mayonnaise
1 teaspoon curry powder
1/4 teaspoon salt
Lettuce leaves

Pour nectar into a medium saucepan. Sprinkle gelatin over nectar; let stand 5 minutes to soften. Cook over low heat, stirring constantly, until gelatin dissolves; remove from heat. In a blender or food processor, puree orange juice and chutney. Add orange-juice mixture to dissolved-gelatin mixture; pour into a 5- to 6-cup ring mold. Refrigerate 4 hours or until firm. In a medium bowl, combine chicken, tangerine, banana, peanuts, mayonnaise, curry powder and salt. Cover and refrigerate. To serve, line a platter with lettuce leaves. Unmold salad onto lettuce-lined platter. Spoon chilled chicken mixture into center of gelatin ring. Makes 6 to 8 servings.

Tip

When shopping for greens, avoid those with dry, yellowing or wilted leaves. Wash leaves gently and shake off as much water as possible. Make sure the leaves are well-drained: pat them with paper towels or spin them in a salad dryer. Then wrap loosely in paper towels or place in a plastic bag. Store in your refrigerator.

Broccoli-Bacon Salad   *Photo on page 28.*

Goes well with sliced meat and cheese at a luncheon buffet.

2 cups chicken stock or bouillon
2 (.25-oz.) envelopes unflavored gelatin
1 tablespoon Worcestershire sauce
1 teaspoon grated onion
1 (10-oz.) pkg. frozen chopped broccoli or
   2 cups chopped fresh broccoli,
   cooked, drained

4 hard-cooked eggs, chopped
4 crisp-cooked bacon slices
1/2 teaspoon salt
1/2 cup mayonnaise
Lettuce leaves
Cherry tomatoes

Pour stock or bouillon in a medium saucepan. Sprinkle with gelatin; let stand 5 minutes to soften. Cook over low heat, stirring constantly, until gelatin dissolves; remove from heat. Stir in Worcestershire sauce and onion. In a blender or food processor, combine broccoli, eggs, bacon, salt and mayonnaise. Cover and process until mixed but not pureed. Stir broccoli mixture into gelatin mixture; pour into a 4-cup mold. Refrigerate until firm. To serve, line a plate or platter with lettuce leaves. Unmold salad onto lettuce leaves. Garnish with cherry tomatoes. Makes 6 servings.

Autumn-Gold Mold

A beautiful addition to your Halloween or Thanksgiving table.

1 (6-oz.) pkg. orange-flavored gelatin
2 cups boiling water
2 persimmons
2 tablespoons lemon juice
1 (8-oz.) can crushed pineapple

1/4 cup coarsely chopped walnuts
Lettuce leaves or curly endive
Orange slices for garnish, if desired
Walnut halves for garnish, if desired

Place gelatin in a medium bowl; pour boiling water over gelatin, stirring until dissolved. Refrigerate until syrupy. Cut persimmons in half; scoop out pulp. In a small bowl or blender, mash or puree persimmon pulp and lemon juice. Stir pureed persimmon mixture, pineapple with juice and chopped walnuts into gelatin mixture; spoon into a 5- to 6-cup mold. Refrigerate 4 hours or until firm. To serve, line a plate with lettuce leaves or curly endive. Unmold salad onto lined plate. Garnish with orange slices and walnut halves, if desired. Makes 6 to 8 servings.

Green-Goddess Dressing

A divine dressing which originated at the Palace Hotel in San Francisco.

3/4 cup mayonnaise
1/2 cup dairy sour cream
1 teaspoon dry mustard
2 tablespoons Tarragon Vinegar, page 44
1 garlic clove, crushed
1/4 teaspoon salt

2 tablespoons finely chopped green onion
2 tablespoons finely chopped watercress
1/4 cup finely chopped fresh parsley
1/8 teaspoon pepper
2 anchovy fillets, finely chopped

In a small bowl, blender or food processor, combine mayonnaise, sour cream and mustard. Add vinegar, garlic, salt, green onion, watercress, parsley, pepper and anchovies. Stir or process until blended. Cover and refrigerate several hours, if possible, before serving. Makes about 1-1/3 cups.

Fresh-Herb Dressing

When fresh herbs are available, try this dressing on a green salad.

1/2 cup dairy sour cream
1/2 cup mayonnaise
2 tablespoons chopped fresh chives
1 tablespoon chopped fresh tarragon
1/4 cup chopped fresh basil
1/4 cup chopped fresh parsley

2 tablespoons white-wine vinegar
1 teaspoon Worcestershire sauce
1/2 teaspoon prepared mustard
1/4 teaspoon pepper
1/2 teaspoon salt
1 garlic clove

Combine all ingredients in a blender or food processor; process until smooth. Store in a covered container in refrigerator. Makes about 1-1/4 cups.

Fruit-Salad Dressing

A great make-ahead time-saver to serve over mixed fresh fruits.

1/4 cup cold water
2 teaspoons unflavored gelatin
1 cup red-wine vinegar
2/3 cup sugar
1/3 cup honey

2 teaspoons celery seed
1 teaspoon salt
1/8 teaspoon pepper
1/4 teaspoon dry mustard

Pour cold water in a medium saucepan. Sprinkle gelatin over water; let stand 5 minutes to soften. Add vinegar, sugar, honey, celery seed, salt, pepper and mustard. Cook over low heat, stirring constantly, until gelatin and sugar dissolve; cool to room temperature. Store in a covered container in refrigerator. Makes about 2 cups.

Dijon Salad Dressing

A light dressing to toss with greens or fresh raw vegetables.

2 tablespoons Dijon-style mustard
2 tablespoons white-wine vinegar
1 egg
1/2 teaspoon Worcestershire sauce
1 teaspoon sugar

2 teaspoons grated Parmesan cheese
1/2 teaspoon salt
1/4 teaspoon pepper
1/2 cup vegetable oil

Combine all ingredients in a small bowl, blender or food processor. Beat or process until blended. Store in a covered container in refrigerator. Makes about 1 cup.

Tip

Because fresh herbs are not available year round, most of these recipes call for dried herbs. Whenever possible, we suggest you use fresh herbs. Usually it is necessary to use about 3 times more fresh than dried.

Fresh-Herb Vinegar   *Photo on page 28.*

Our favorite herb combination for salad vinegar.

2 tablespoons chopped fresh basil leaves
2 tablespoons chopped fresh celery leaves
1 tablespoon chopped fresh thyme leaves
1 teaspoon mustard seeds

1 garlic clove, cut in half
2 cups white-wine vinegar or
   distilled white vinegar

In a glass pint jar, combine basil, celery and thyme leaves. With edge of a wooden spoon, gently bruise leaves. Add mustard seeds, garlic and vinegar. Cover with paper towel; let stand at room temperature 5 to 7 days. Strain through 2 thicknesses of cheesecloth or a very fine sieve; discard herbs. Pour vinegar into a clean pint jar; seal with a screw top or cork. Label jar and store in refrigerator. Makes about 2 cups.

Tarragon Vinegar

If you substitute distilled white vinegar for white-wine vinegar, the flavor will be less pleasing.

1/4 cup chopped fresh tarragon leaves
2 cups white-wine vinegar

Place tarragon in a glass pint jar. With edge of a wooden spoon, gently bruise leaves; add vinegar. Cover with paper towel; let stand at room temperature 5 to 7 days. Strain through 2 thicknesses of cheesecloth or a very fine sieve; discard leaves. Pour vinegar into a clean pint jar; seal with a screw top or cork. Label jar and store in refrigerator. Makes about 2 cups.

Variation
Instead of using tarragon leaves, substitute 1/4 cup chopped fresh dill, basil, green onion or shallots, oregano or other fresh herbs.

Chili Vinegar

Lends a south-of-the-border flavor to sauces and salads.

2 jalapeño peppers
2 cups white-wine vinegar or
   distilled white vinegar

Wash, dry and remove stem from peppers. Split peppers in half lengthwise; remove and discard seeds. Place pepper halves in a clean pint jar; add vinegar. Cover with paper towel; let stand at room temperature 5 to 7 days. Remove and discard pepper halves. Seal with a screw top or cork. Label jar and store in refrigerator. Makes about 2 cups.

 Tip
When chopping green onions, use all the white portion and about 2 inches of the tender green portion.

Pasta & Pizza

Pasta is an extremely important part of California cuisine. Served hot or cold, it is paired with vegetables to make salads or with cheese and meat for main dishes.

KINDS OF PASTA

Pasta encompasses more than noodles served with pot roast or spaghetti crowned with a tomato sauce. There's an endless variety of shapes. As a rule, the smallest shapes are used for soups and salads. Our favorites for salads include capellini, vermicelli, small elbow macaroni, fettucini and small shell macaroni. Before cooking long pasta shapes for salads, break them into 2- to 3-inch lengths.

Some pastas, such as fettucini, may be used as the base for both salads and main dishes. Lasagne noodles, large shells, large elbow macaroni and rigatoni are popular for main dishes.

If you enjoy making your own pasta, your family or guests are sure to appreciate your efforts. Homemade pasta is generally more delicate than commercial types.

WAYS WITH PASTA

In Italy, pasta is a separate course served before the meat course. Here there are no rigid rules for serving pasta. Sometimes you can coat pasta with butter, cheese and herbs, then serve it as a separate course or a side dish. Another time you may create a main dish, such as Ranch-Style Fettucini, a healthy combination of vegetables and cheese with pasta. For a change of pace, show off our White Lasagne, teaming chicken and ham with cheese.

California's love affair with salads has spread to pasta. Antipasto Pasta Salad is hearty enough to become the main dish at lunch or an appetizer before an important dinner. The new trend in California restaurants is reflected in Avant-Garde Pasta Salad.

PIZZA TRENDS

Exciting new pizza ideas are making a splash in cooking circles. Instead of traditional combinations, the emphasis is on fresh products. Replacing the tomato-sauce base are fresh tomatoes marinated in oil and herbs. Thinly sliced pear-shaped Italian tomatoes marinated in olive oil and fresh basil or tarragon make a great topping. Or, use regular tomatoes in oil with dried herbs.

Topping the fresh-tomato base are different combinations. Try New-Wave Topping using smoked duck, fennel, orange pieces and Monterey Jack cheese. For a special event, serve Caviar Topping, caviar, hard-cooked egg, ricotta and Monterey Jack cheeses and dill weed. The dessert pizza is sure to create quite a stir. Make ours—or make your own combination. ❖

Avant-Garde Pasta Salad

An up-to-date salad, similar to those offered at several restaurants.

5 to 6 oz. uncooked vermicelli or capellini
1 lb. fresh asparagus spears
1 small jícama, peeled, cut in
   matchstick pieces
4 oz. California goat cheese, diced
1 tablespoon Tarragon Vinegar, page 44
1 tablespoon lemon juice

1 tablespoon chopped shallots or
   green onion
2 teaspoons Dijon-style mustard
1/4 teaspoon salt
1/8 teaspoon pepper
1/4 cup olive oil or vegetable oil
1/4 cup toasted pine nuts

Cook vermicelli or capellini according to package directions; drain. Pour cold water over pasta; let stand while preparing salad. Break off and discard about 2 inches of the tough end of each asparagus spear. Cut asparagus in 1-inch pieces. Steam or cook asparagus in a small amount of water until tender; drain and cool. Drain vermicelli or capellini. In a large salad bowl, combine cooked asparagus spears, cooked pasta, jícama and cheese. In a blender or food processor, combine vinegar, lemon juice, shallots or green onion, mustard, salt and pepper; process until smooth. With blender or processor motor still running, slowly add oil. Process until blended. Pour vinegar mixture over asparagus mixture; toss to coat well. Sprinkle pine nuts over top. Serve immediately, or refrigerate until serving time. Makes 5 to 6 servings.

Antipasto Pasta Salad

A glamorous, make-ahead, meal-in-one salad with an Italian accent.

8 oz. uncooked small shell macaroni
1/2 lb. fresh or frozen asparagus spears
1 cup Italian salad dressing
2 green onions, sliced
2 cups cherry tomatoes, cut in halves

2 oz. thinly sliced pepperoni
1 cup diced mild or sharp Cheddar cheese
   (4 oz.)
Lettuce leaves

Cook macaroni according to package directions; drain. Pour cold water over macaroni; let stand while preparing salad. If using fresh asparagus, break off and discard about 2 inches of the tough end of each asparagus spear. Cut asparagus in 1-inch pieces. Steam or cook asparagus in a small amount of water until tender; drain and cool. Drain cooked macaroni. In a large bowl, combine drained macaroni, cooked asparagus pieces, Italian dressing, green onions and cherry tomatoes. Cover; refrigerate at least 2 hours. Stir mixture at least once, if possible. Before serving, cut pepperoni slices in halves; add pepperoni and cheese to salad. Toss to blend. Line a large bowl or platter with lettuce leaves. Spoon salad into lettuce-lined bowl or platter. Serve immediately. Makes 6 to 8 servings.

Tip
_____

Shelled almonds are sold whole or sliced unblanched, as well as blanched whole or slivered. Small cans of flavored almonds, such as barbecue, garlic or cheese, are handy for snacks.

Garden Pasta Salad

Best when served immediately after tossing together.

4 oz. uncooked fettucini
1 zucchini, thinly sliced
1 cup cherry tomatoes, cut in halves
1/2 cup thinly sliced radishes
2 carrots, thinly sliced
1/4 cup dairy sour cream

1/4 cup mayonnaise
1/4 teaspoon dried dill weed
1 teaspon salt
1/4 teaspoon pepper
1/4 teaspoon garlic salt

Break fettucini in 3-inch pieces. Cook according to package directions; drain. Pour cold water over fettucini; let stand while preparing salad. In a large bowl, combine zucchini, tomatoes, radishes and carrots. Drain fettucini; add to vegetables. In a small bowl, combine sour cream, mayonnaise, dill weed, salt, pepper and garlic salt. Pour sour-cream mixture over vegetables; toss until well blended. Serve immediately. Makes 5 to 6 servings.

Marina-Shell Salad

Impressive addition to a salad buffet.

1 cup uncooked small pasta shells
2 tablespoons prepared horseradish
1/3 cup bottled chili sauce
1 tablespoon lemon juice
2 tablespoons chopped green onion
1/2 teaspoon salt
1/4 teaspoon pepper

2 tablespoons prepared mustard
1/2 cup dairy sour cream
2 cups cooked crabmeat (12 oz.)
3 hard-cooked eggs, chopped
Lettuce leaves
Ripe olives for garnish
Cherry tomatoes for garnish

Cook pasta shells according to package directions; drain. Pour cold water over pasta; let stand while preparing salad. In a medium bowl, combine horseradish, chili sauce, lemon juice, green onion, salt, pepper, mustard and sour cream. Add crabmeat and eggs. Drain cooked pasta; toss with crab mixture. Arrange lettuce leaves on a platter or individual salad plates; top with pasta mixture. Garnish with ripe olives and cherry tomatoes. Serve immediately. Makes 6 to 8 servings.

California-Style Pesto

Great to prepare when you have lots of fresh basil.

2 cups loosely packed fresh basil leaves
1/4 cup chopped fresh parsley
1/3 cup walnuts or almonds
1 garlic clove
1/3 cup olive oil

1/2 teaspoon salt
1/8 teaspoon pepper
1/4 cup butter
8 oz. uncooked spaghetti or fettucini
1/2 cup grated Parmesan cheese (1-1/2 oz.)

In a blender or food processor, combine basil leaves, parsley, nuts, garlic, olive oil, salt, pepper and butter. Process until mixture is nearly smooth. Cook spaghetti or fettucini according to package directions; drain. Place cooked pasta in a large serving bowl. Stir cheese into basil mixture; pour over cooked pasta. Toss lightly. Serve immediately. Makes 5 to 6 servings.

Ranch-Style Fettucini

Fettucini is delicious as a separate pasta course or main dish.

1/2 cup butter or margarine
2 zucchini, cut in matchstick pieces
1 carrot, cut in matchstick pieces
1/4 lb. sliced fresh mushrooms
1/4 cup sliced green onions
1/2 teaspoon dried leaf basil

1/2 teaspoon salt
1/8 teaspoon pepper
1 cup cooked green peas
8 oz. uncooked fettucini
1/2 cup grated Parmesan cheese (1-1/2 oz.)

Melt butter or margarine in a medium skillet over medium heat. Add zucchini and carrot; sauté until nearly tender. Stir in mushrooms, green onions, basil, salt and pepper; cook 2 minutes. Add peas; cook until hot. Cook fettucini according to package directions; drain. Add cheese and cooked vegetables to fettucini; toss lightly. Serve immediately. Makes 5 to 6 servings.

Variation

To make this a one-dish meal, add 1-1/2 cups chopped cooked ham.

White Lasagne

A great do-ahead dish.

1/4 cup butter or margarine
1 small onion, chopped
1/3 cup all-purpose flour
2 cups chicken stock or bouillon
1-1/2 cups milk or half and half
1/2 teaspoon salt
1/8 teaspoon pepper
1 tablespoon minced fresh parsley

1/4 cup dry white wine
8 oz. uncooked lasagne noodles
1 cup diced cooked turkey or chicken
8 oz. sliced mozzarella cheese
2 cups diced cooked ham
1/2 cup grated Parmesan
    cheese (1-1/2 oz.)

Melt butter or margarine in a medium saucepan over medium heat. Add onion; sauté until soft. Stir in flour. Cook, stirring constantly, until bubbly. Pour in stock or bouillon and milk or half and half. Stir over medium-low heat until slightly thickened. Add salt, pepper, parsley and wine; remove from heat. Grease a 13'' x 9'' baking pan. Cook lasagne noodles in boiling salted water until tender; drain. Preheat oven to 350F (175C). Arrange about 1/3 of cooked noodles on bottom of greased pan; top with 1 cup turkey or chicken, 1/3 of cream sauce and 1/3 of sliced cheese. Make a second layer of 1/3 of cooked noodles; top with 2 cups ham, 1/3 of sauce and 1/3 of sliced cheese. Make a third layer of remaining cooked noodles; top with cream sauce and sliced cheese. Sprinkle with grated cheese. Bake 30 to 40 minutes or until bubbly. Serve hot. Makes 6 to 8 servings.

Cannery Row Tetrazzini

A California version of a traditional pasta dish.

1/4 cup butter or margarine
1/4 cup all-purpose flour
1-1/2 cups chicken stock or bouillon
1 cup half and half
1 cup sliced fresh mushrooms
4 to 6 oz. cooked artichoke hearts, chopped
1/2 teaspoon salt
1/8 teaspoon pepper
1/8 teaspoon ground nutmeg

3 tablespoons dry white wine
2 (6-1/2-oz.) cans oil- or water-pack tuna, drained
1/2 cup shredded Monterey Jack cheese (2 oz.)
6 oz. uncooked spaghetti
1/2 cup grated Parmesan cheese (1-1/2 oz.)
Sliced pitted ripe olives, if desired

Preheat oven to 350F (175C). In a medium saucepan, melt butter or margarine; stir in flour. Cook 2 minutes over medium heat. Stir in stock or bouillon and half and half. Cook, stirring constantly, until slightly thickened. Add mushrooms, artichoke hearts, salt, pepper and nutmeg. Cook, stirring constantly, 1 minute. Stir in wine, tuna and Monterey Jack cheese. Cook spaghetti according to package directions; drain. Combine cooked spaghetti and tuna mixture. Spoon into a shallow 2-1/2-quart baking dish. Sprinkle with Parmesan cheese. Bake 20 to 30 minutes or until bubbly. Garnish with ripe olives, if desired. Serve hot. Makes 6 servings.

Home-Style Pasta

A good basic sauce for everything from main-dish spaghetti to lasagne.

1 tablespoon vegetable oil
1/2 lb. bulk pork sausage, crumbled
1 lb. boneless beef chuck or round, cut in 1/2-inch pieces
1 onion, chopped
1 carrot, chopped
1 garlic clove, crushed
1 teaspoon salt

1/4 teaspoon pepper
1 teaspoon dried leaf oregano, crushed
1/2 teaspoon dried leaf basil
1 (16-oz.) can tomatoes with juice, cut-up
1 (6-oz.) can tomato paste
8 oz. uncooked egg-noodle bows or corkscrews
Grated Parmesan cheese

Heat oil in a large heavy saucepan over medium heat. Add sausage and beef; brown on all sides. Add onion, carrot and garlic; sauté until vegetables are soft. Stir in salt, pepper, oregano, basil, tomatoes and tomato paste. Cover and simmer about 2 hours. Cook noodles according to package directions; drain. Place cooked noodles on a large platter. Spoon tomato sauce over cooked noodles; sprinkle cheese over noodles and sauce. Serve immediately. Makes 6 servings.

Tip

To toast almonds, arrange a single layer of blanched whole, slivered or chopped almonds in a shallow baking pan. Heat in 350F (175C) oven 5 to 10 minutes or until desired color is obtained.

Buffet Pasta Bar

Salad bars are very popular, so let's try a pasta bar. Use the same principle as for a salad bar.

Here's the basic idea. Set up a buffet where guests can help themselves to a basic pasta such as fettucini. Let guests choose Bolognese Topping, Béchamel Topping or half of each. Then top with as many accessory foods, listed below, as they choose.

Cook fettucini or other pasta as close to serving time as possible. Allow 2 ounces uncooked pasta per person. Drain well and toss with vegetable oil or butter. Keep it hot in the top of a steamer or colander over hot water. If possible, keep both toppings hot in chafing dishes, slow cookers or in bowls on a hot tray.

ACCESSORY FOODS

Cooked chopped bacon	Sliced mushrooms
Sliced cooked artichoke hearts	Slivered cooked chicken
Shredded raw carrot	Thinly sliced pepperoni
Chopped raw broccoli	Sliced ripe olives
Shredded raw zucchini	Crumbled blue or Gorgonzola cheese
Shredded Monterey Jack cheese	Grated Parmesan cheese
Jicama in matchstick pieces	Shredded raw crookneck squash
Cooked green peas	Slivered red and green bell pepper

Pasta-Bar Bolognese Topping

2 tablespoons vegetable oil	1 teaspoon salt
2 tablespoons butter	1/4 teaspoon pepper
1 onion, chopped	1/2 teaspoon dried leaf basil
1 carrot, chopped	1 tablespoon minced fresh parsley
1 celery stalk, chopped	1 cup dry white wine
1 lb. lean ground beef	1/2 cup milk
1/2 lb. mild Italian sausage	1/8 teaspoon ground nutmeg
1 (28-oz.) can Italian tomatoes with juice, chopped	

Heat oil and butter in a 4-quart saucepan over medium heat. Sauté onion, carrot and celery 2 to 3 minutes. Stir in ground beef and sausage. Cook, stirring until meat loses its red color and is crumbly. Stir in tomatoes, salt, pepper, basil, parsley and wine. Cook over medium-high heat, uncovered, 30 minutes or until reduced by 2/3. Reduce heat; stir in milk and nutmeg. Cook, stirring constantly, 5 minutes longer. Serve hot. Makes 6 to 8 servings.

Pasta-Bar Béchamel Topping

1/2 cup butter or margarine	1/2 teaspoon prepared mustard
1/2 cup all-purpose flour	1/2 teaspoon Worcestershire sauce
1 qt. (4 cups) milk or half and half	1/2 cup grated Parmesan cheese
1/2 teaspoon salt	(1-1/2 oz.)
1/8 teaspoon pepper	

In a medium saucepan, melt butter or margarine. Add flour; cook, stirring constantly, 2 minutes. Add milk or half and half, salt, pepper, mustard and Worcestershire sauce. Cook over low heat, stirring constantly, 2 to 3 minutes or until thickened. Stir in Parmesan cheese. Serve hot. Makes 5 to 6 servings.

How to Make Individual Pizza

1/Arrange topping over each 6-inch circle of dough.   2/Garnish each baked pizza with dill weed or as desired.

Individual Pizza

Choose your favorite topping with this pizza.

1 cup warm water (105F, 40C)
1 (1/4-oz.) pkg. (1 tablespoon) active
   dry yeast
1 teaspoon sugar

1 teaspoon salt
2 tablespoons vegetable oil
3 to 3-1/4 cups all-purpose flour
Choice of topping, opposite

Pour water in a medium bowl. Sprinkle yeast over water; stir until dissolved. Let stand about 5 minutes. Stir in sugar, salt, oil and 1 cup flour; beat well. Add additional flour, about 2 cups, to make a soft dough. Turn out on a lightly floured board. Knead dough 15 times, working in enough flour to make a stiff dough. Clean and grease bowl. Place dough in bowl; turn to grease top. Cover and let rise in a warm place 40 to 45 minutes or until doubled in size. Preheat oven to 425F (220C). Punch down dough to remove air. Divide dough in 6 equal parts. Pat each portion into a 5- to 6-inch circle on a baking sheet. Pinch edge to form a shallow rim around each circle. Add choice of topping. Bake 15 to 20 minutes or until golden brown. Makes 6 servings.

Pizza Toppings

Hacienda Topping:
In a medium bowl, combine 1/4 cup olive oil and 1 (4-ounce) can diced green chilies, drained. Add 4 sliced fresh Italian-style tomatoes; marinate 1 hour. Drain tomatoes and chilies. Top uncooked pizzas with drained tomato slices and chilies, 3/4 cup julienned cooked chicken, 1/3 cup sliced pitted ripe olives, 2 tablespoons sliced green onion and 1 cup shredded Monterey Jack cheese. Bake as directed. After baking, garnish each pizza with avocado slices.

Chinatown Topping:
In a medium bowl, combine 2 tablespoons sesame oil, 1/4 cup vegetable oil, 2 tablespoons minced crystallized ginger and 1 teaspoon grated orange peel. Add 4 sliced fresh Italian-style tomatoes; marinate 1 hour. Top uncooked pizzas with drained tomato slices and ginger, 3 ounces pea pods, 3/4 cup thinly sliced water chestnuts, 3/4 cup cooked shelled small shrimp, 2 tablespoons sliced green onion and 3/4 cup shredded Monterey Jack cheese. Bake as directed.

New-Wave Topping:
In a medium bowl, combine 1/3 cup olive oil and 2 table spoons fresh tarragon or 2 teaspoons dried leaf tarragon. Add 4 sliced fresh Italian-style tomatoes; marinate 1 hour. Top uncooked pizzas with drained tomato slices, 1-1/2 cups julienned smoked turkey or duck, 1 cup thinly sliced uncooked fennel, 1 peeled orange cut in bite-size pieces and 1 cup shredded Monterey Jack cheese. Bake as directed.

California-Goat-Cheese Topping:
In a medium bowl, combine 1/3 cup olive oil and 2 tablespoons fresh tarragon or 2 teaspoons dried leaf tarragon. Add 4 sliced fresh Italian-style tomatoes; marinate 1 hour. Top uncooked pizzas with drained tomato slices, 3 ounces thinly sliced California goat cheese, 12 sliced mushrooms and 1/4 cup grated Parmesan cheese. Bake as directed.

Barbecued-Fish Topping:
Thinly slice 1 leek; separate slices into rings, making about 2 cups. In a medium bowl, toss leek rings with 1/4 cup olive oil. Let stand about 1 hour. Top uncooked individual pizzas with 2 ounces shredded Monterey Jack cheese, 3 ounces California goat cheese cut in 1/2-inch pieces, 3 ounces slivered barbecued salmon or albacore and marinated leeks. Sprinkle with 1/4 cup grated Parmesan cheese, if desired. Bake as directed. Sprinkle with fresh chopped dill or dried dill weed.

Caviar Topping:
In a medium bowl, combine 1/3 cup olive oil and 2 teaspoons dried leaf basil. Add 4 sliced fresh Italian-style tomatoes; marinate 1 hour. Top uncooked pizzas with drained tomato slices; 4 sliced hard-cooked eggs, 1/4 cup red, black or golden caviar, 1/2 cup ricotta cheese and 1 cup shredded Monterey Jack cheese. Bake as directed.

Vegetarian Topping:
In a medium bowl, combine 1/3 cup olive oil and 2 teaspoons dried leaf basil. Add 4 sliced fresh Italian-style tomatoes; marinate 1 hour. Top uncooked pizzas with drained tomato slices; 12 thinly sliced mushrooms; 1 zucchini, shredded; 1 carrot, shredded; 3/4 cup cooked garbanzo beans and 1 cup shredded Monterey Jack cheese. Bake as directed. After baking, garnish each pizza with alfalfa sprouts.

Dessert Pizza:
Top uncooked pizzas with 3/4 cup flaked coconut; 2 small bananas, thinly sliced; 2 small pears, peeled and thinly sliced; 3/4 cup shredded white chocolate and 1/3 cup melted butter combined with 1/3 cup chopped walnuts. Bake as directed.

Breads

reads of California are a reflection of many ethnic groups. Thanks to the Mexican influence, tortillas have always been an important part of the cuisine. They serve a dual purpose—that of a bread or as the main ingredient for popular dishes such as tacos or enchiladas. Both corn and flour tortillas are readily available in California markets. If you have trouble finding them in your area or if you prefer homemade, we have included recipes for both. To heat tortillas, wrap a stack of them in foil. Heat in a 350F (175C) oven 15 minutes or until hot. In a microwave, stack tortillas in a plastic bag with several slits in it. Heat 45 seconds to 1-1/2 minutes, depending on the number of tortillas.

SOURDOUGH BREADS

Apparently sourdough breads were brought to our part of the country by early settlers. Old stories of the Gold Rush Days sometimes mention sourdough biscuits or flapjacks. The old-timers guarded their *starters* and were always careful to replace the amount they used. Today, San Francisco sourdough bread is world-famous. Visitors to the city want to taste this special bread. Restaurants and grocery stores offer it in large round loaves with flat tops, in addition to the traditional French loaf. At major California airports, you can purchase a loaf of San Francisco sourdough as a souvenir.

In the last few years, there has been a great interest in bread baking at home. You can take pride in presenting a crunchy loaf of fragrant hot bread to family or friends. In this chapter, we've included Sourdough Starter. It must stand several days before you use it—plan ahead so it will be ready when you are. If sourdough is a new experience, try the Sourdough English Muffins first. You'll love the results. Then progress to Sourdough Bread.

Don't neglect the other recipes. In both yeast and non-yeast categories, we offer a variety of ideas using different grains. Californians have always been interested in good nutrition. Even before the physical-fitness programs spread throughout the country, whole grains were popular here. Whole-wheat flour, cracked wheat and sunflower nuts give texture and flavor to breads and muffins.

Flour used in our bread recipes was not sifted. Carefully spoon flour into a clean dry measuring cup. Level off with a knife, being careful not to pack it. All-purpose flour is used for recipes requiring white flour—with one exception. The Pronto Beer Bread calls for self-rising flour; do not substitute other flours. Self-rising flour has leavening in it, making it possible to get results in a short time. This old recipe is always well received because of its unusual flavor and time-saving qualities. ❖

California Health Bread   *Photo on page 63.*

Loaded with foods that are good for you.

1 cup whole-wheat flour	**2 eggs, slightly beaten**
1/4 cup wheat germ	**1/2 cup honey**
1 cup all-purpose flour	**1 cup plain yogurt**
1 teaspoon baking soda	**1/4 cup butter, melted**
2 teaspoons baking powder	**1/2 cup chopped dates**
1/2 teaspoon salt	

Preheat oven to 325F (165C). Grease a 9'' x 5'' loaf pan; set aside. In a large bowl, stir together whole-wheat flour, wheat germ, all-purpose flour, baking soda, baking powder and salt. In a medium bowl, combine eggs, honey, yogurt, butter and dates; add to dry mixture. Stir until blended. Pour mixture into greased pan. Bake 40 to 50 minutes or until a wooden pick inserted in center comes out clean. Cool in pan 10 minutes. Turn bread out onto a cooling rack. Serve warm or cool. Makes 1 loaf.

Oatmeal-Raisin Bread

Delicious hot or cold; however, it's easier to slice when cool.

1 cup rolled oats, regular or quick-cooking	**1/2 teaspoon ground cinnamon**
1 cup all-purpose flour	**2 eggs, slightly beaten**
1 teaspoon baking soda	**1/3 cup molasses**
1-1/2 teaspoons baking powder	**1 cup buttermilk**
1/2 teaspoon salt	**2 tablespoons vegetable oil**
1/2 cup raisins	**1 tablespoon rolled oats**
1/4 cup chopped walnuts	

Preheat oven to 350F (175C). Grease a 9'' x 5'' loaf pan; set aside. In a large bowl, combine 1 cup rolled oats, flour, baking soda, baking powder, salt, raisins, walnuts and cinnamon. In a medium bowl, combine eggs, molasses, buttermilk and oil; add to dry mixture. Stir until blended. Spoon mixture into greased pan. Sprinkle with 1 tablespoon rolled oats. Bake 50 minutes or until a wooden pick inserted in center comes out clean. Cool in pan 10 minutes. Turn bread out onto a cooling rack. Serve warm or cool. Makes 1 loaf.

Pronto Beer Bread

Be sure to use self-rising flour.

3 cups self-rising flour	**1 (12-oz.) can beer**
3 tablespoons sugar	**1/3 cup butter, melted**

Preheat oven to 375F (190C). Grease 2 (8'' x 5'') loaf pans. In a medium bowl, combine flour and sugar; gradually stir in beer. Spoon mixture into greased pans. Drizzle butter over top of each loaf. Bake 45 to 50 minutes or until golden brown. Turn breads out onto cooling racks. Serve warm. Makes 2 loaves.

Western-Style Sour-Cream Coffeecake

Select your favorite combination of dried fruits.

3/4 cup butter or margarine,
  room temperature
1-1/2 cups sugar
2 eggs
1 teaspoon vanilla extract
2 teaspoons baking powder
1/2 teaspoon baking soda
1/2 teaspoon salt

2-1/4 cups all-purpose flour
1 cup dairy sour cream
1/4 cup chopped walnuts
1/2 cup chopped dates, prunes or dried figs
1/4 cup diced dried peaches or apricots
1/2 teaspoon ground cinnamon
2 tablespoons sugar

Preheat oven to 350F (175C). Grease and flour a 10-inch tube pan. In a large bowl, cream together butter or margarine and 1-1/2 cups sugar. Add eggs; beat until light. Mix in vanilla, baking powder, baking soda, salt and half the flour. Add sour cream; beat until smooth. Beat in remaining flour. Stir in walnuts; dates, prunes or figs; and peaches or apricots. Spread batter in greased pan. In a small bowl, combine cinnamon and 2 tablespoons sugar; sprinkle mixture over batter. Bake 45 minutes. Cool in pan 15 minutes. Serve warm or cool with cinnamon-sugar side up. Makes 8 to 10 servings.

Upside-Down Plum Muffins   *Photo on page 63.*

A delicious fruit muffin for breakfast, brunch or coffee hour.

1/4 cup butter or margarine, melted
3 tablespoons sugar
1/4 teaspoon ground cinnamon
6 small plums, cut in thirds
1 egg
1 cup milk

1/4 cup vegetable oil
2 cups all-purpose flour
1 tablespoon baking powder
1/4 cup sugar
1/4 teaspoon salt

Preheat oven to 400F (205C). Grease 12 muffin cups; set aside. Spoon 1 teaspoon melted butter or margarine into each muffin cup. In a small bowl or measuring cup, combine 3 tablespoons sugar with cinnamon; sprinkle over butter or margarine in each muffin cup. Place a plum third in each muffin cup. In a medium bowl, beat egg; add milk and oil. Stir in flour, baking powder, 1/4 cup sugar and salt until flour is moistened—avoid over-mixing. Spoon over plums. Bake 20 to 25 minutes or until golden brown. Immediately invert on a cooling rack. Cool 1 minute; remove muffin pan. Serve warm. Makes 12 muffins.

Tip
_____

For variety, substitute slices of fresh peaches or nectarines for plums.

Triple-Wheat Muffins

Cracked wheat gives a nutty flavor and chewy texture.

1 cup whole-wheat flour	**1/2 teaspoon salt**
1 cup all-purpose flour	**1 egg, slightly beaten**
1/4 cup cracked wheat	**1 cup buttermilk**
1 teaspoon baking soda	**2 tablespoons vegetable oil**
1 teaspoon baking powder	**2 tablespoons honey**

Preheat oven to 375F (190C). Line 12 muffin cups with fluted paper liners, or grease 12 muffin cups; set aside. In a large bowl, combine whole-wheat flour, all-purpose flour, cracked wheat, baking soda, baking powder and salt. In a medium bowl, combine egg, buttermilk, oil and honey. Add egg mixture to flour mixture; stir enough to moisten dry ingredients—avoid over-mixing. Spoon into prepared muffin cups. Bake 15 to 20 minutes or until golden brown and a wooden pick inserted in center comes out clean. Serve warm. Makes 12 muffins.

Autumn Muffins

Super brunch fare.

1 egg, slightly beaten	**1/2 teaspoon ground cinnamon**
1/2 cup milk	**1/4 teaspoon ground nutmeg**
1/4 cup lightly packed brown sugar	**1/4 teaspoon ground allspice**
1/4 cup butter or margarine, melted	**1-3/4 cups all-purpose flour**
2/3 cup cooked or canned pumpkin	**1 tablespoon baking powder**

Preheat oven to 400F (205C). Line 12 muffin cups with fluted paper liners, or grease 12 muffin cups; set aside. In a medium bowl, combine egg, milk, brown sugar, butter or margarine, pumpkin, cinnamon, nutmeg and allspice. In a small bowl, combine flour and baking powder; add to egg mixture. Stir enough to moisten dry ingredients—avoid over-mixing. Spoon into prepared muffin cups. Bake 20 to 25 minutes or until golden brown. Serve warm. Makes 12 muffins.

Double-Apple Pancakes

For a special crunch, sprinkle chopped walnuts over the top.

1 cup applesauce	**1 tart apple, peeled, finely chopped**
1 tablespoon brown sugar	**2 tablespoons raisins**
1/4 teaspoon ground cinnamon	**1 cup pancake mix**
1/8 teaspoon ground ginger	**3 tablespoons butter or margarine, melted**
2 eggs, beaten	**2 tablespoons powdered sugar**
1 cup milk	**3/4 cup dairy sour cream**

In a small bowl, combine applesauce, brown sugar, cinnamon and ginger; set aside. In a medium bowl, combine eggs, milk, apple and raisins. Stir in pancake mix and butter or margarine. Preheat a griddle. For each pancake, pour about 1/4 cup batter on hot griddle. Bake until golden brown on both sides. Spoon about 1 tablespoon applesauce mixture on each pancake; fold over. Spoon powdered sugar into a small strainer; sprinkle over filled pancakes. Top each pancake with 1 tablespoon sour cream. Serve immediately. Makes about 12 (4- to 5-inch) pancakes.

Sourdough Starter

Store starter in a glass or ceramic container.

2-1/2 cups warm water (110F, 45C)   2 cups all-purpose flour
1 (1/4-oz.) pkg. (1 tablespoon)   1 tablespoon sugar
   active dry yeast

Pour 1/2 cup water in a large glass or ceramic bowl. Sprinkle yeast over water; stir to dissolve yeast. Stir in remaining water, flour and sugar; beat until smooth. Loosely cover mixture; let stand in a warm place 3 to 4 days or until bubbly. Stir 2 or 3 times each day. Loosely cover and refrigerate until needed. After using 1 to 1-1/2 cups starter, add 3/4 cup water, 3/4 cup all-purpose flour and 1 teaspoon sugar to remaining starter. Let stand at room temperature 1 day or until bubbly. Loosely cover and refrigerate until needed. Continue to *feed* starter by adding water, flour and sugar to remaining starter after removing some starter for baking. If a clear liquid forms on top, stir back into starter. Makes 3 to 4 cups.

Sourdough French Bread

Create your own San Francisco sourdough with this recipe.

1 cup Sourdough Starter, above   1/2 cup warm water (110F, 45C)
1 cup warm water (110F, 45C)   1 (1/4-oz.) pkg. (1 tablespoon)
2 teaspoons sugar   active dry yeast
2 teaspoons salt   Milk
5-1/2 to 6 cups all-purpose flour

In a large bowl, combine sourdough starter, 1 cup warm water, sugar, salt and 3 cups flour; beat until blended. Cover with a damp towel, followed by foil. Let stand at room temperature 6 hours or until mixture has doubled in size. In a second large bowl, pour 1/2 cup water. Sprinkle yeast over water; stir until dissolved. Let stand 5 minutes. Add sourdough mixture; beat well. Stir in 1 cup flour or enough to make a very stiff dough. Turn out on a lightly floured board. Knead in as much flour as dough will absorb. Clean and grease bowl. Place dough in bowl; turn to grease top. Cover and let rise in a warm place 1-1/2 hours or until doubled in size. Punch down dough to remove air. Let dough rise again about 45 minutes. Grease a baking sheet. Divide dough in 2 equal portions. Shape each portion in a 14'' x 3'' loaf. Place on greased baking sheet, 3 inches apart. With a sharp knife, make 4 or 5 (1/2-inch-deep) diagonal slashes on top of each loaf. Cover and let rise 1 hour or until doubled in size. Preheat oven to 400F (205C). Place a shallow pan of hot water on lower oven rack. Place baking sheet with bread on middle oven rack. Bake 35 to 40 minutes. Remove from baking sheet; brush lightly with milk. Cool on wire racks. Makes 2 loaves.

How to Make Sourdough English Muffins

1/Sprinkle ungreased baking sheets with cornmeal. Place muffins 2 inches apart on sheets and let rise.

2/Cook muffins over medium heat on a lightly greased griddle or an electric griddle.

Sourdough English Muffins

A real treat and easy to make.

3/4 cup milk
3 tablespoons sugar
1 teaspoon salt
2 tablespoons butter or margarine
1/4 cup warm water (110F, 45C)

1 (1/4-oz.) pkg. (1 tablespoon)
  active dry yeast
1-1/2 cups Sourdough Starter, opposite
4 to 5 cups all-purpose flour
Cornmeal

In a medium saucepan, heat milk, sugar, salt and butter or margarine until butter or margarine melts; cool slightly. Pour water in a large bowl. Sprinkle yeast over water; stir until dissolved. Let stand 5 minutes. Add warm milk mixture, sourdough starter and 2-1/2 cups flour; beat until smooth. Stir in enough additional flour to make a stiff dough. Turn out on a lightly floured board. Knead 2 minutes or until dough can be formed into a ball. Clean and grease bowl. Place dough in bowl; turn to grease top. Cover and let rise in a warm place 1 hour or until doubled in size. Punch down dough to remove air. Divide dough in half. Roll out half of dough on a lightly floured board to 1/2 inch thickness. Cut dough with a floured 3-inch-round cookie cutter. Sprinkle ungreased baking sheets with cornmeal. Place muffins, 2 inches apart, on baking sheets. Repeat with remaining dough. Cover and let rise in a warm place 30 minutes or until doubled in size. With a metal spatula, place muffins, cornmeal-side down, on a lightly greased griddle. Cook over medium heat, or on an electric griddle with control set at about 300F (150C). Bake 8 to 10 minutes on each side. To serve, split in half and toast. Makes 16 muffins.

Green-Chili Cornbread

So soft and tender that it resembles spoonbread.

1 cup cornbread mix
2 eggs, beaten
1/4 cup butter or margarine, melted
1 cup dairy sour cream

1 cup fresh, frozen or
   drained canned whole-kernel corn
1 (4-oz.) can diced green chilies, drained
2 cups shredded Cheddar cheese (8 oz.)

Preheat oven to 350F (175C). Grease an 8-inch square pan; set aside. In a medium bowl, combine cornbread mix, eggs, butter or margarine and sour cream; stir until blended. Stir in corn and green chilies. Pour half the mixture into greased pan. Sprinkle 1 cup cheese over top. Top with remaining batter followed by remaining cheese. Bake 40 minutes or until golden brown. Serve warm. Makes 6 to 8 servings.

Homemade Corn Tortillas

Masa harina is a corn mixture sold in gourmet stores or supermarkets.

2 cups masa harina
1-1/4 to 1-1/2 cups warm water (110F, 45C)

In a medium bowl, combine masa harina with enough water to hold dough together. Using your hands, form mixture into a small ball. Divide dough in 12 pieces. If you have a tortilla press, put a square of plastic wrap or waxed paper on bottom half of press; top with ball of dough almost in center of press, but slightly toward front edge. Top with a second square of plastic wrap or waxed paper. Flatten slightly with hand. Press down firmly with handle of press until tortilla is about 6 inches in diameter. Repeat with remaining dough. Stack tortillas with waxed paper or plastic wrap between each. If you don't have a tortilla press, use a rolling pin to roll out each ball between waxed paper or plastic wrap. To cook, peel off top paper. Turn tortilla over on an ungreased hot griddle or skillet. Peel off other paper as tortilla heats and softens. Cook about 1 minute or until it looks dry. Turn several times. Tortilla should be soft, but dry with a few light-brown spots. Makes 12 servings.

Flour Tortillas

Lard is the traditional fat used in making Mexican tortillas.

1/3 cup lard or shortening
3 cups all-purpose flour

1 teaspoon salt
3/4 cup room-temperature water

In a medium bowl, combine lard or shortening, flour and salt. Using a pastry blender or a fork, cut lard or shortening into flour until crumbs are about the size of peas. Stir in water to make a stiff dough. Knead on a lightly floured board about 1 minute or until smooth. Divide dough in 18 pieces. Cover and let stand 15 minutes. Roll each ball into a 7-inch circle. Bake on a medium-hot ungreased griddle about 1 minute on each side or until firm and with golden-brown spots. Serve hot. Makes 18 servings.

Tip
_____

Flour tortillas are easy to roll with a rolling pin. Corn tortillas are more difficult to roll, so it is easier to use a press.

How to Make Monkey Bread

1/Cut dough circles; dip each in butter or margarine. Arrange in 3 layers in pan.

2/Remove bread from baking pan. Pull bread apart and serve warm or cool.

Monkey Bread

A popular, pull-apart bread that originated in California.

1/4 cup warm water (110F, 45C)	1 tablespoon sugar
1 (1/4-oz.) pkg. (1 tablespoon) active dry yeast	2 eggs, slightly beaten
3/4 cup milk	1 teaspoon salt
1/4 cup butter or margarine	2-1/2 to 3 cups all-purpose flour
	1/2 cup butter or margarine, melted

Butter a 10-inch tube pan; set aside. Pour water in a large bowl. Sprinkle yeast over water; stir until dissolved. Let stand 5 minutes. In a small saucepan, heat milk, 1/4 cup butter or margarine and sugar until butter is nearly melted; cool slightly. Add warm-milk mixture, eggs and salt to dissolved yeast. Beat in 2 cups flour. Add enough remaining flour to form a soft dough. Cover and let rise in a warm place about 1 hour or until doubled in size. Roll dough, half at a time, on a lightly floured board to 1/4 inch thickness. Cut into 3-inch circles. Dip each round in melted butter or margarine. Arrange in 3 overlapping layers in greased pan. Cover and let rise in a warm place 30 minutes or until doubled in size. Preheat oven to 400F (205C). Bake 35 minutes or until golden brown. Cool in pan 5 minutes. Remove from baking pan. Pull apart to serve, either hot or cool. Makes 20 to 22 pull-apart rolls.

Fiesta Bread

A casserole-type bread which is at its best when served fresh from the oven.

1/4 cup warm water (110F, 45C)
1 (1/4-oz.) pkg. (1 tablespoon)
  active dry yeast
1/2 cup milk
1 teaspoon salt
1/2 cup vegetable oil
1 teaspoon sugar

3 eggs
2-3/4 cups all-purpose flour
1/2 cup finely chopped ripe olives
1 tablespoon finely chopped pimiento
2 tablespoons finely chopped green onion
1 cup shredded Monterey Jack cheese
  (4 oz.)

Grease a round 2-quart baking dish; set aside. Pour water in a large bowl. Sprinkle yeast over water; stir until dissolved. Let stand 5 minutes. Scald milk by heating in a small saucepan over low heat until bubbles appear around the edge; cool slightly. To yeast mixture, add warm milk, salt, oil, sugar, eggs and half the flour. Beat at medium speed 3 minutes. Stir in remaining flour, olives, pimiento, green onion and cheese. Cover and let rise in a warm place 45 to 60 minutes or until doubled in size. Stir batter down; spoon into greased baking dish. Cover and let rise 45 to 60 minutes or until doubled in size. Preheat oven to 375F (190C). Bake 40 to 45 minutes or until loaf sounds sounds hollow when tapped with your fingers. Cut into wedges and serve warm. Makes 1 round loaf.

Sunflower-Wheat Bread

A short-cut recipe with a heavy batter that should be beaten rather than kneaded.

1/2 cup warm water (110F, 45C)
2 (1/4-oz.) pkgs. (2 tablespoons)
  active dry yeast
1 cup milk
1/4 cup molasses

1/4 cup shortening
1 teaspoon salt
2 cups all-purpose flour
1 cup whole-wheat flour
1/2 cup unsalted sunflower nuts

Grease a 10-inch tube pan; set aside. Pour water in a large bowl. Sprinkle yeast over water; stir until dissolved. Let stand 5 minutes. In a small saucepan, heat milk, molasses, shortening and salt until shortening is nearly melted; cool slightly. Add warm milk mixture to dissolved yeast; stir in all-purpose flour and whole-wheat flour. Reserve 2 tablespoons sunflower nuts; add remaining nuts to batter. Beat until blended. Cover and let rise in a warm place 50 to 60 minutes or until doubled in size. Preheat oven to 375F (190C). Stir batter down; beat about 1/2 minute. Spoon batter into greased pan. Sprinkle with reserved 2 tablespoons sunflower nuts. Bake 35 minutes. Cool in pan 5 minutes. Remove from baking pan and cool completely on a rack. Makes 1 (10-inch) round loaf.

Tip
_____

Don't expect breads made with a high percentage of whole wheat, oats or cracked wheat to rise as high as bread made with white flour.

California Health Bread, page 55; Fiesta Bread, above; Upside-Down Plum Muffins, page 56; and Bits-of-Gold Marmalade, page 73.

Flaky Croissants

Well worth the effort, but be sure to allow plenty of time to make them.

3/4 cup milk	2 tablespoons vegetable oil
1 tablespoon sugar	3 cups all-purpose flour
1 teaspoon salt	2 sticks butter (1 cup)
1/4 cup warm water (110F, 45C)	1 egg yolk, beaten
1 (1/4-oz.) pkg. (1 tablespoon)	1 tablespoon water
active dry yeast	

In a small saucepan, heat milk, sugar and salt, stirring until sugar dissolves; cool. Pour 1/4 cup warm water in a small bowl; stir in yeast to dissolve. In a large bowl, combine milk mixture, yeast mixture, oil and 1 cup flour; beat until smooth. Stir in remaining flour. Turn out dough on a lightly floured surface. Knead 12 or 15 times or to form a smooth ball. Clean and grease bowl. Place dough in bowl; turning to grease dough. Cover and let rise at 70F (20C) 2-1/2 hours or until tripled in size. Punch down dough; cover and let rise again until doubled in size or about 1 hour. While dough is rising, shape butter on waxed paper into 2 (7" x 3") rectangles. Cover and refrigerate until firm. On a lightly floured surface, roll out dough to a 12" x 8" rectangle. If necessary, turn dough so 8-inch edges are at top and bottom. With a knife, lightly score the rectangle into thirds across narrow part. Place 1 rectangle of butter in center of top third of dough. Place another rectangle of butter in center third of dough. Fold bottom third of dough without butter over center third of dough. Fold top third over that. Rotate dough so open side of flap is on the right. On a lightly floured surface, carefully roll dough to 12" x 8" rectangle. Fold in thirds again. Wrap in plastic wrap; refrigerate 30 to 40 minutes. Repeat rolling, folding and chilling process. Roll dough to a 12" x 8" rectangle; fold into thirds again. This makes 3 times to roll, fold and chill. Wrap and refrigerate at least 1 hour. Cut dough in half, crosswise. Refrigerate half of dough while rolling other half to a 12-inch round. Cut into 6 wedges. Starting with rounded edge, gently roll each wedge toward the tip. Slightly stretch dough as you roll it. Shape in crescent with points turned toward you. Place tip down, about 2 inches apart, on an ungreased baking sheet. Repeat with other dough half. In a small bowl, combine egg yolk and 1 tablespoon water. Brush shaped dough with egg-yolk mixture. Cover and let rise at 65F (20C) or a cool place about 3-1/2 to 4 hours or until doubled. Preheat oven to 400F (205C). Bake in upper third of oven 5 minutes. Reduce heat to 350F (175C); bake 15 to 20 minutes or until golden. Makes 12 croissants.

Variation

Short-Cut Croissants: In a small saucepan, heat milk, sugar and salt, stirring until sugar dissolves; cool. Pour 1/4 cup warm water in a small bowl; stir in yeast to dissolve. In a food processor fitted with a steel blade, combine milk mixture, yeast mixture, oil and 1 cup flour; turn processor on and off 3 to 4 times. Add remaining flour; process 30 seconds or until dough forms a ball. Turn out dough on a lightly floured surface. Knead into a flattened ball about 6 inches across. Wrap in plastic wrap; refrigerate 45 minutes. Cut butter in 30 slices; cover and freeze. Cut chilled dough in 15 pieces. Place 5 pieces chilled dough and 10 slices butter in food processor. Turn processor on and off 20 to 30 times or until butter is evenly distributed. Refrigerate. Repeat twice with remaining dough and butter. Combine 3 batches of dough; press together. On a lightly floured surface, roll out dough to a 16" x 6" rectangle. If necessary, turn dough so 6-inch edges are at top and bottom. Fold top 4 inches of dough down over next 4-inch section. Bring bottom 4 inches of dough up over next 4-inch section. Then, fold top 2 layers over bottom 2 layers, forming a stack of 4 dough layers. Wrap and refrigerate 15 to 20 minutes. Repeat rolling and refrigerating 3 additional times. After final rolling, cut dough in half, wrap and freeze 30 minutes. Refrigerate half of dough while rolling and shaping as above, letting dough rise 1-1/2 to 2 hours at 70 to 75F (20 to 25C). Bake as described above.

How to Make Croissants

1/Place butter in center of top third of dough and in center third of dough. Fold bottom third of dough without butter over center third of dough.

2/Roll half the dough to a 12-inch round. Cut round into 6 pie-shaped wedges. Starting with rounded edge, gently roll each wedge toward the tip.

Croissant Fillings

Each of the croissant fillings makes enough for 6 croissants. Fill croissants just before rolling the pie-shaped dough pieces. Spread 1 to 1-1/2 tablespoons desired filling about 1/2 inch inside rounded edge. Roll and shape as recipe directs.

Almond Paste: Stir together 1/3 cup almond paste, 1 tablespoon butter, 1 tablespoon flour and 1 tablespoon powdered sugar. Top unbaked croissants with sliced almonds.

Cheese-Fruit: Stir together 1/3 cup ricotta cheese, 2 tablespoons finely chopped raisins, 1 tablespoon finely chopped dried apricots, 1/4 teaspoon grated orange peel and 1 teaspoon flour.

Herbed Cheese: Stir together 3/4 cup shredded Swiss cheese, 1/2 teaspoon dried dill weed, 1/2 teaspoon dried parsley and 1/4 teaspoon instant minced onion.

Tropical: Stir together 1/4 cup finely chopped dates, 1 tablespoon finely chopped walnuts, 2 tablespoons coconut, 1 teaspoon melted butter and 1 teaspoon flour.

Chocolate: 1/2 cup semisweet chocolate pieces or 1 ounce grated white chocolate.

Smoky Barbecue Rolls

A yeast bread that doesn't keep you in the kitchen all day.

3/4 cup warm water (110F, 45C)
1 (1/4-oz.) pkg. (1 tablespoon)
  active dry yeast
2 tablespoons sugar
1 teaspoon salt
2 tablespoons smoky barbecue sauce

1 tablespoon minced fresh chives
1/4 teaspoon dried leaf marjoram
1 egg
2 tablespoons shortening
2-1/4 cups all-purpose flour

Pour water in a large bowl. Sprinkle yeast over water; stir until dissolved. Let stand 5 minutes. Stir in sugar, salt, barbecue sauce, chives, marjoram, egg, shortening and 1 cup flour; beat until smooth. Stir in remaining flour until smooth. Cover; let rise in warm place 30 minutes or until doubled in size. Grease 12 muffin cups. Stir down batter. Beat about 25 strokes; spoon into greased muffin cups. Let stand 20 minutes or until doubled in size. Preheat oven to 400F (205C). Bake rolls 15 minutes. Makes 12 rolls.

Garden-Vegetable Wheat Braids

What a pleasant surprise to discover vegetables inside the braid!

1 cup milk
3 tablespoons honey
2 teaspoons salt
1/4 cup shortening
1/4 cup warm water (110F, 45C)
1 (1/4-oz.) pkg. (1 tablespoon)
  active dry yeast
2 cups all-purpose flour
1-3/4 to 2 cups whole-wheat flour
2 tablespoons butter or margarine

1 garlic clove, minced
1/4 cup chopped green onions
1/4 cup chopped celery
1 small carrot, finely chopped
1 cup chopped zucchini
1/2 teaspoon salt
1/8 teaspoon pepper
1/2 teaspoon dried leaf oregano
1/4 cup grated Parmesan cheese (3/4 oz.)
Milk

In a medium saucepan, heat 1 cup milk, honey, salt and shortening until shortening melts; cool slightly. Pour water in a large bowl. Sprinkle yeast over water; stir until dissolved. Let stand 5 minutes. Stir in warm milk mixture. Add half the all-purpose flour and half the whole-wheat flour; beat until smooth. Stir in remaining all-purpose flour and enough whole-wheat flour to make a stiff dough. Turn out on a lightly floured board; knead 5 to 8 minutes or until smooth and elastic. Clean and grease bowl. Place dough in bowl; turn to grease top. Cover and let rise in a warm place 1-1/4 hours or until doubled in size. While bread is rising, melt butter or margarine in a medium skillet over medium heat. Add garlic, green onions, celery, carrot and zucchini; sauté until tender. Add salt, pepper and oregano. Cover and cook over low about 5 minutes. Drain; cool to room temperature. Grease a large baking sheet. Punch down dough to remove air. Turn out on a lightly floured board. Divide dough in half. Roll half of dough in an oblong about 14" x 7". Spread half the sautéed vegetables down center of bread. Top with half the cheese. Cut 13 diagonal slits in dough along each side of filling, makes 14 strips about 1 inch wide. Fold strips at an angle across filling, alternating from side to side. Place on greased baking sheet. Repeat with remaining dough. Cover and let rise in a warm place 50 to 60 minutes or until doubled in size. Preheat oven to 350F (175C). Brush top of bread with milk. Bake 30 to 35 minutes or until loaf sounds hollow when tapped with your fingers. Serve warm or cool. Makes 2 (14-inch) braids.

Armenian Cracker Bread

An ideal accompaniment for soups and salads.

1-1/2 cups warm water (110F, 45C)
1 (1/4-oz.) pkg. (1 tablespoon)
  active dry yeast
1 teaspoon salt

3-1/2 to 4 cups all-purpose flour
Water, room temperature
1/4 cup sesame seeds

Pour water in a large bowl. Sprinkle yeast over water; stir until dissolved. Let stand 5 minutes. Stir in salt and enough flour to make a stiff dough. Turn out dough on a lightly floured board. Knead 5 to 8 minutes or until smooth and elastic. Clean and grease bowl. Place dough in bowl; turn to grease top. Cover and let rise in warm place 1-1/2 hours or until doubled in size. Punch down dough to remove air. Cover and let rise until doubled again, about 30 to 45 minutes. Preheat oven to 400F (205C). Pinch off pieces of dough about 1-1/2 inches in diameter. Roll each piece of dough on a lightly floured board until very thin or about an 8-inch round. Brush with water; sprinkle with sesame seeds. Bake, 2 at a time, on a 17" x 14" baking sheet 15 to 20 minutes or until lightly browned and puffy. Makes 26 to 28 breads.

How to Make Garden-Vegetable Wheat Braids

1/Cut 13 diagonal slits, about 1-inch apart, in dough along each side of filling.

2/Fold strips at an angle across filling, alternating from side to side. Pinch ends closed.

Cracked-Wheat Bread

Multi-wheat ingredients provide a very pleasant, nut-like flavor.

1/4 cup warm water (110F, 45C)
2 (1/4-oz.) pkgs. (2 tablespoons)
  active dry yeast
1/4 cup honey
1-3/4 cups milk

1/4 cup butter or margarine, melted
2 teaspoons salt
1/2 cup cracked wheat
2 cups whole-wheat flour
3 to 3-1/3 cups all-purpose flour

Grease 2 (8-1/2" x 4-1/2") loaf pans; set aside. Pour water in a small bowl or measuring cup. Sprinkle yeast over water; stir until dissolved. Let stand 5 minutes. In a large bowl, combine honey, milk, butter or margarine, salt, cracked wheat, whole-wheat flour and dissolved yeast; beat until smooth. Beat in enough all-purpose flour to make a stiff dough. Turn out on a lightly floured board. Knead 5 to 8 minutes or until smooth. Add more all-purpose flour, if needed, to prevent dough from sticking. Clean and grease bowl. Place dough in bowl; turn to grease top. Cover and let rise in a warm place 1-1/2 hours or until doubled in size. Punch down dough to remove air. Turn out on a lightly floured board; knead dough lightly. Divide dough in 2 equal pieces; shape into 2 loaves. Place loaves in greased pans. Cover and let rise 45 minutes or until doubled in size. Preheat oven to 375F (190C). Bake 40 to 45 minutes or until loaf sounds hollow when tapped with your fingers. Cool 5 to 10 minutes in pans. Remove from baking pans and cool completely on racks. Makes 2 loaves.

Jalapeño-Cheese Bread

Vary the number of jalapeño peppers according to how hot you like it.

1 or 2 fresh jalapeño peppers
1 cup warm water (110F, 45C)
1 (1/4-oz.) pkg. (1 tablespoon)
  active dry yeast
1 tablespoon sugar
1 teaspoon salt
2 tablespoons butter or margarine,
  room temperature

1 tablespoon instant minced onion
1/4 teaspoon garlic salt
1 egg, beaten
1 cup shredded Cheddar cheese (4 oz.)
3 to 3-1/2 cups all-purpose flour

Grease a round 9-inch cake pan; set aside. Remove stem and cut jalapeño peppers in halves; scoop out and discard seeds. Finely chop pepper; set aside. Pour water in a large bowl. Sprinkle yeast over water; stir until dissolved. Let stand 5 minutes. Stir in sugar, salt, butter or margarine, onion, garlic salt, egg, cheese, 2 cups flour and chopped jalapeño peppers; beat until blended. Stir in enough remaining flour to make a soft dough. Turn out on a lightly floured board; knead 5 to 8 minutes or until smooth and elastic. Clean and grease bowl. Place dough in bowl; turn to grease top. Cover and let rise in a warm place 1 hour or until doubled in size. Punch down dough to remove air. Turn out on a lightly floured board. Knead dough lightly until smooth. Shape dough in a ball; place in greased pan. Cover and let rise in a warm place 45 minutes or until doubled in size. Preheat oven to 425F (220C). Bake 25 minutes or until loaf sounds hollow when tapped with your fingers. If top gets too brown, loosely cover with foil last 10 minutes of baking. Serve warm. Makes 1 (9-inch) round loaf.

Vegetables

The Mid-West has always been known as the breadbasket of the country because of its bountiful crops of wheat and corn. Likewise, California could be labeled the "vegetable basket" of America. Fertile valleys throughout the state produce their own specialties, depending on the soil, temperature and amount of water.

Thanks to moderate year-round weather, it is often possible to grow two or more crops of the same vegetable. Some vegetables, such as tomatoes, are grown in different climates within the state. First, they ripen in the warmer area. About the time the crop is finished there, tomatoes begin to ripen in a more-moderate climate. Thus, the overall season is extended.

Everyone benefits from the extended fresh vegetable supply. All of us are eating more vegetables than before. Years ago, vegetables were not emphasized and their use was limited. Now, we use them in every part of the meal from appetizers to desserts. If you have a tendency to fix vegetables the same way day after day, break the monotony and try our suggestions.

STUFFED VEGETABLES

Shells of many vegetables make interesting, tasty edible containers for all kinds of entrees or vegetable combinations. Scoop out and par-boil green peppers, zucchini or onions. Fill with a delicious assortment of foods such as corn, cheese or tomatoes, and season with herbs and spices. Crumbled crackers, breadcrumbs or grated cheese make interesting toppings. Fresh artichokes lend themselves to this treatment. Chicken-Stuffed Artichokes make an impressive beginning for a dinner party. They take slightly longer to prepare but the compliments you receive will make it worth your efforts.

VEGETABLES & STIR-FRYING

Stir-frying is a technique borrowed from the Chinese. Its greatest appeal is the speed with which it is done. Use your wok or a large skillet. The secret is to have vegetables cut in uniform pieces. Then, cook quickly at a high temperature in a small amount of oil. Garden-Fresh Stir-Fry is a colorful combination that will convert even the most reluctant vegetable-eaters.

THINK FRESH

It's hard to beat the taste and nutritive value of fresh raw vegetables. Unrivaled in popularity as dippers are carrot sticks and celery hearts. Less well known, but equally good, are jicama or turnip rounds, cauliflower or broccoli flowerets, and fennel or crookneck-squash slices. Dieters will appreciate these low-calorie choices on your menu.❖

Fresh Artichokes

Basic directions for trimming, cooking and serving.

6 fresh artichokes　　　　　　　　　**2 tablespoons lemon juice**
2 teaspoons salt

Slice about a 1-inch piece off the top of each artichoke. Cut off stem near base. With scissors, trim about 1/2 inch off tip of each leaf. Pour water 2 to 3 inches deep in an 8-quart pot; add salt and lemon juice. Bring seasoned water to a boil. Carefully add artichokes, 1 at a time. Cover and simmer 25 to 35 minutes or until a leaf can be easily pulled from artichoke. Remove artichokes; drain, upside-down, in a colander 1 to 2 minutes. Serve 1 artichoke per person. If possible, serve each artichoke on an individual salad plate with a small cup of dipping sauce on the side. To eat, pull out leaves, 1 at a time, dipping base of each leaf in sauce. Eat the tender green base of each leaf by pulling it between your teeth. Discard the tough part of each leaf. Continue pulling leaves out until you get to the fuzzy center or *choke*. With a spoon or knife, scrape choke out and discard it. The remaining part is the most tender and flavorful portion: the *artichoke bottom*. Cut the bottom with a knife. Using a fork, dip pieces in the sauce and eat them. Makes 6 servings.

Lemon-Butter Sauce:
1/2 cup butter or margarine　　　　　　**1/2 teaspoon seasoned salt**
1/4 cup lemon juice

In a small saucepan, melt together butter or margarine, lemon juice and seasoned salt. Divide in 6 individual custard cups or small saucers. Keep warm until ready to serve.

Curry Mayonnaise:
1 cup mayonnaise　　　　　　　　　**1/4 teaspoon salt**
1 teaspoon curry powder

In a small bowl, combine mayonnaise, curry powder and salt. Divide in 6 individual custard cups or small saucers. Set aside until ready to serve.

Stir-Fried Asparagus

An idea borrowed from traditional Chinese cooking.

2 lbs. fresh asparagus spears　　　　　**1/4 cup chicken stock or bouillon**
2 tablespoons butter　　　　　　　　　**1/4 teaspoon salt**
1 tablespoon vegetable oil　　　　　　**1/8 teaspoon pepper**
1 teaspoon soy sauce　　　　　　　　**2 tablespoons toasted slivered almonds**
1 teaspoon lemon juice

Break off and discard about 2 inches of the tough end of each asparagus spear. Cut spears, diagonally, in 1/4-inch slices. Heat butter and oil in a 10-inch skillet; add asparagus slices. Cook, stirring over medium-high heat, 2 minutes. Stir in soy sauce, lemon juice, stock or bouillon, salt and pepper. Cover and cook 2 to 3 minutes longer or until tender. Sprinkle with almonds. Serve hot. Makes 5 to 6 servings.

How to Prepare Artichokes

1/Slice off about a 1-inch piece from the top of each artichoke.

2/Using scissors, trim off about 1/2 inch from the tip of each leaf.

Chicken-Stuffed Artichokes

For added flavor, top with a dab of chutney.

6 fresh artichokes
1 teaspoon salt
1/4 cup butter or margarine
2 green onions, chopped
1/4 cup all-purpose flour
1/2 teaspoon salt
1/8 teaspoon pepper
1 teaspoon curry powder

1/2 teaspoon Worcestershire sauce
1 cup half and half
1 cup chopped cooked chicken
1/2 cup chopped mushrooms
2 tablespoons dry white wine
1/4 cup soft breadcrumbs
1/4 cup finely chopped blanched almonds

Cut artichokes in half crosswise; discard top half. Trim about 1/2 inch off tip of each leaf. Cut stem off at base. Pour water 2 to 3 inches deep in a 4- to 5-quart pot; add 1 teaspoon salt. Bring water to a boil. Carefully add artichoke halves, 1 at a time. Cover and simmer 20 minutes or until tender. Remove artichokes; drain, upside-down, on paper towels. Preheat oven to 350F (175C). With a spoon, scoop out choke. In a medium saucepan, melt butter or margarine. Add green onions; sauté 2 to 3 minutes. Stir in flour, salt, pepper, curry powder and Worcestershire sauce. Pour in half and half. Cook, stirring constantly, until thickened. Stir in chicken, mushrooms and wine; spoon into drained artichoke halves. In a small bowl, combine breadcrumbs and almonds; sprinkle over stuffed artichokes. Bake 20 to 30 minutes or until tops are golden. Serve hot. Makes 6 servings.

Commuter's Broccoli-Bake

Easy, yet good-tasting for after-work entertaining.

2 lbs. fresh broccoli
Salt and pepper
2 tablespoons butter or margarine, melted
1/2 teaspoon Worcestershire sauce
1/4 teaspoon salt

1/8 teaspoon pepper
1/2 cup soft breadcrumbs
3 tablespoons butter or margarine, melted
1/4 cup grated Parmesan cheese (3/4 oz.)
1/8 teaspoon paprika

Cut off and discard tough ends from broccoli stalks. Cut large stalks in half lengthwise. Steam or cook broccoli in a small amount of water to crisp-tender stage; drain. Preheat broiler. Arrange cooked broccoli in a shallow 1-1/2-quart baking dish. Season broccoli with salt and pepper. In a small bowl, combine 2 tablespoons melted butter or margarine, Worcestershire sauce, 1/4 teaspoon salt and 1/8 teaspoon pepper. Pour butter or margarine mixture over broccoli. In a small bowl, combine breadcrumbs, 3 tablespoons melted butter or margarine, cheese and paprika. Spoon crumb mixture over broccoli. Broil broccoli mixture, 4 inches from heat, 2 to 3 minutes or until topping is golden brown. Serve hot. Makes 4 to 5 servings.

Ranch-Style Broccoli

Bacon brings out the best in broccoli.

2 lbs. fresh broccoli
4 bacon slices, finely chopped
2 tablespoons butter or margarine
1/4 cup all-purpose flour
1 cup chicken stock or bouillon
1 cup milk

1/4 teaspoon salt
1/8 teaspoon pepper
1 teaspoon Worcestershire sauce
Paprika
1 hard-cooked egg, finely chopped

Cut off and discard tough ends from broccoli stalks; chop remaining broccoli. Steam or cook chopped broccoli in a small amount of water to crisp-tender stage; drain and set aside. In a small skillet, cook bacon until crisp. Reserve 2 tablespoons bacon drippings. In a medium saucepan, melt butter or margarine. Stir in reserved bacon drippings and flour until blended and bubbly; remove from heat. Add stock or bouillon, milk, salt, pepper and Worcestershire sauce. Cook, stirring over medium heat, until thick and smooth. Stir in drained cooked broccoli and cooked bacon. Heat through, but do not boil. Spoon into a serving dish. Sprinkle with paprika. Garnish with hard-cooked egg. Serve hot. Makes 6 servings.

Sweet-Sour Carrots

A different flavor treatment for carrots.

6 medium carrots
1/4 cup butter or margarine
1/4 teaspoon salt

1/4 cup lightly packed brown sugar
1/4 cup Burgundy
1/2 teaspoon grated orange peel

Cut carrots in 1/4-inch diagonal slices. Melt butter or margarine in a 9-inch skillet. Add carrot slices; sauté 2 minutes. Add salt, brown sugar, Burgundy and orange peel. Cover and simmer 10 to 15 minutes or until tender. Serve hot. Makes 4 servings.

Carrot-Ring Soufflé

For a colorful serving effect, fill center of ring with cooked peas and mushrooms.

1/2 cup butter or margarine
1/2 cup lightly packed brown sugar
3 egg yolks
2 cups mashed cooked carrots
    (about 8 carrots)
1/4 teaspoon salt

1 cup all-purpose flour
1/2 teaspoon baking powder
1/2 teaspoon baking soda
1/4 cup orange juice
1 teaspoon grated orange peel
3 egg whites

Preheat oven to 350F (175C). Grease a 6-cup ring mold. In a large bowl, cream together butter or margarine and brown sugar. Beat in egg yolks and carrots. Add salt, flour, baking powder, baking soda, orange juice and orange peel. In a medium bowl, beat egg whites until stiff but not dry. Fold beaten egg whites into carrot mixture. Spoon carrot mixture into greased mold. Place filled mold in a 13'' x 9'' baking pan. Pour 3 cups boiling water around mold in baking pan. Bake 40 to 50 minutes or until firm. Let stand in pan with hot water 5 minutes. Run a small spatula around sides of mold. Invert on a platter. Serve immediately. Makes 6 to 8 servings.

Stir-Fried Carrots

Colorful, tasty and good for you.

6 medium carrots
2 tablespoons butter or margarine
1 tablespoon vegetable oil

2 tablespoons orange juice
2 tablespoons brown sugar
1/8 teaspoon ground nutmeg

Cut carrots in 1/8-inch diagonal slices. In a medium skillet, heat butter or margarine and oil. Add carrot slices; cook, stirring over medium-high heat, 3 minutes. Add orange juice, sugar and nutmeg. Cover and cook 2 to 4 minutes or until crisp-tender. Serve hot. Makes 5 to 6 servings.

Bits-of-Gold Marmalade   *Photo on page 63.*

Your guests will never guess that carrots are in this recipe.

5 tangerines
1/3 cup lemon juice
2 large carrots, shredded

5 cups sugar
1 (3-fl. oz.) foil pkg. liquid pectin

Wash 5 (1/2-pint) jars in hot soapy water; rinse. Keep jars hot until needed. Prepare lids as manufacturer directs. Peel tangerines; remove and discard stringy membrane. Cut peel in julienne strips about 1 inch long and 1/8 inch wide. In a medium saucepan, cover peel with water. Cover and simmer 30 minutes; drain. Cut fruit in 1/2-inch pieces; discard seeds. In a 6- to 8-quart pan, combine drained cooked peel, fruit pieces, lemon juice, carrots and sugar. Bring to a full rolling boil, stirring occasionally. Boil hard 3 minutes, stirring constantly. Stir in pectin. Bring back to a full rolling boil; boil 1 minute longer. Skim foam from surface. Ladle hot marmalade into 1 hot jar at a time, leaving 1/4-inch headspace. Wipe rim of jar with a clean damp cloth. Attach self-sealing lid. Repeat with remaining jars. Place filled jars on a rack in a large pot of boiling water. Water should cover jars 1 to 2 inches and have an additional 2 inches for boiling space. Cover pot. Bring water back to a boil. At sea level, boil 10 minutes. For every 1000 feet altitude, add 1 minute to boiling time. Store up to 1 year. Makes 4 to 5 (1/2-pint) jars.

Pacifica Brussels Sprouts

For a change of pace, add a few marinated Brussels sprouts to a favorite green salad.

3/4 to 1 lb. small Brussels sprouts
2 tablespoons finely chopped dill pickle
2 tablespoons finely chopped pimiento
2 tablespoons finely chopped green onion
1/4 cup dry white wine

2 tablespoons vegetable oil
1 garlic clove, crushed
1 teaspoon honey
1/2 teaspoon salt
1/4 teaspoon pepper

Trim Brussels sprouts; cut in half lengthwise. Steam or cook Brussels sprouts in a small amount of water until tender but firm; drain and cool. In a medium bowl, combine pickle, pimiento, green onion, wine, oil, garlic, honey, salt and pepper. Add drained cooked Brussels sprouts. Cover and refrigerate at least 1 hour. Drain and serve as a cold vegetable accompaniment to roasts or barbecued meats. Makes 4 to 6 servings.

Chicken-Leek Soup

Even better than mother's traditional chicken soup.

2 lbs. chicken wings
6 cups water
1 carrot, finely chopped
1 celery stalk, finely chopped
2 tablespoons minced fresh parsley

1 teaspoon salt
1/4 teaspoon pepper
1/4 teaspoon dried red-pepper flakes
3 leeks

In a large saucepan, combine chicken wings, water, carrot, celery, parsley, salt, pepper and red-pepper flakes. Cook over medium heat 20 to 30 minutes or until chicken is tender. Remove chicken; when cool enough to handle, remove and discard bones and skin. Return chicken to saucepan. Cut off and discard dark-green leek tops. Cut each leek lengthwise in quarters; wash thoroughly to remove any sand. Cut leeks crosswise in 1/2-inch slices. Add to chicken mixture. Simmer 8 to 10 minutes or until leeks are tender. Serve warm. Makes 6 to 7 servings.

Leeks à la Suisse

Don't overlook this quick-to-fix, yet elegant dish.

6 leeks
1 cup chicken stock or bouillon
2 bacon slices, chopped
1/2 teaspoon salt

1/8 teaspoon pepper
1/3 cup grated Swiss cheese (1-1/2 oz.)
3 tablespoons soft breadcrumbs

Cut off and discard dark-green leek tops. Cut each leek lengthwise in half; wash thoroughly to remove any sand. In a large skillet, combine leeks, stock or bouillon, bacon, salt and pepper. Cover and simmer 10 minutes or until leeks are tender; drain. Preheat broiler. Place cooked leeks and bacon in a broiler pan. In a small bowl, combine cheese and breadcrumbs. Sprinkle cheese mixture over leeks. Broil, 4 inches from heat, 1 minute or until cheese melts. Serve hot. Makes 6 servings.

Tip

Be sure to wash leeks thoroughly to eliminate the sand trapped between layers.

Pacifica Brussels Sprouts with Lemon-Tree Chicken, page 121.

Brie-Topped Cauliflower

Make ahead, then broil at the last minute.

1 medium head cauliflower	1/4 teaspoon salt
1/4 cup butter or margarine	1/8 teaspoon pepper
1/4 cup all-purpose flour	1/2 cup chopped California Brie
1 cup chicken stock or bouillon	cheese (4 oz.)
1 cup milk	

Break cauliflower in flowerets. Steam or cook in water until barely tender; drain and set aside. Preheat broiler. In a small saucepan, melt butter or margarine. Stir in flour until blended and bubbly; remove from heat. Stir in stock or bouillon, milk, salt and pepper. Cook, stirring over medium heat, until thick and smooth. Add cheese, stirring until melted. In a shallow 2-quart baking dish, combine cauliflower and cheese sauce. Broil, 6 inches from heat, 2 minutes or until bubbly and lightly browned. Serve hot. Makes 4 to 5 servings.

Cauliflower Soup

A very smooth and tasty soup.

1 medium head cauliflower	1/4 cup butter or margarine
2 cups chicken stock or bouillon	2 tablespoons all-purpose flour
1 small onion, chopped	1 cup half and half
1/2 teaspoon salt	1/8 teaspoon ground mace
1/8 teaspoon pepper	Croutons

Cut cauliflower in bite-size flowerets. In a medium saucepan, combine cauliflowerets, stock or bouillon, onion, salt and pepper. Cover and cook 10 minutes or until tender. In a blender or food processor, puree cooked cauliflower mixture until smooth. In a medium saucepan, melt butter or margarine. Stir in flour; cook, stirring constantly, until flour becomes a light-golden color. Add half and half, mace and cauliflower mixture. Heat through, but do not boil. Pour into individual soup bowls. Sprinkle with croutons. Serve immediately. Makes 4 to 5 servings.

Variation

Substitute 1/4 cup chopped green onions for small onion. To serve, sprinkle with croutons and 1 tablespoon chopped green onion.

Creative Ways With Grapefruit

Cut each grapefruit in half crosswise. Using a sharp knife or grapefruit knife, cut around membrane on outside edges as well as between each segment.

To Serve Cold: Spoon 1 tablespoon of your choice of the following over each grapefruit half.
- Raspberry liqueur
- Crème de Menthe
- Maraschino-cherry juice

To Serve Hot: Spoon your choice of the following over each grapefruit half. Broil 2 to 3 minutes until topping begins to bubble and brown. Serve immediately.
- 1 tablespoon maple-flavored syrup
- 1 tablespoon red cinnamon candy
- 1 teaspoon each finely chopped dates, flaked coconut and brown sugar
- 1 tablespoon Burgundy topped with 1 tablespoon red-currant jelly

Fresh Cream-of-Pea Soup

Looks fresh, tastes fresh, is fresh!

1/4 cup butter or margarine	1/8 teaspoon pepper
1 carrot, finely chopped	1/2 teaspoon fines herbes
1 small onion, finely chopped	1/8 teaspoon ground mace
2 cups chicken stock or bouillon	1 teaspoon sugar
2 cups fresh green peas or	1/4 cup all-purpose flour
1 (10-oz.) pkg. frozen green peas	1/3 cup water
1/2 teaspoon salt	2 cups half and half

In a large saucepan, melt butter or margarine; add carrot and onion. Sauté until onion is soft. Add stock or bouillon, peas, salt, pepper, fines herbes, mace and sugar; cook until peas are tender. In a blender or food processor, puree half the mixture at a time. Return pureed mixture to saucepan. In a small bowl, combine flour and water. Stir flour mixture into pureed mixture. Cook over medium heat, stirring until thickened. Stir in half and half. Serve warm. Makes 6 servings.

Spinach-Stuffed Mushrooms

To serve as appetizers, use small mushrooms.

1 (10-oz.) pkg. frozen chopped spinach or	1 hard-cooked egg, chopped
1 bunch fresh spinach	1 teaspoon prepared mustard
12 to 14 large mushrooms (2-inch diameter)	1/2 teaspoon salt
2 tablespoons butter or margarine	1/8 teaspoon pepper
1 garlic clove, crushed	2 tablespoons mayonnaise
1 teaspoon Worcestershire sauce	1/4 cup grated Parmesan cheese (3/4 oz.)

Cook frozen spinach according to package directions. Or, wash fresh spinach to remove any sand. Place spinach in a medium saucepan with a small amount of water. Cook over medium heat 2 to 5 minutes. Drain cooked spinach in a sieve; press out excess water with back of spoon; set aside. Remove mushroom stems; finely chop stems. In a medium skillet, melt butter or margarine. Add chopped mushroom stems and garlic. Sauté until stems are soft; remove from heat. Add Worcestershire sauce, hard-cooked egg, mustard, salt, pepper, mayonnaise, cheese and drained cooked spinach. Preheat oven to 350F (175C). Spoon some spinach mixture into each mushroom cap. Place each mushroom, stuffed-side up, in an 11" x 7" shallow baking pan. Pour 3/4 cup hot water in bottom of pan, being careful not to pour water on mushrooms. Bake 20 minutes or until mushrooms are hot. Remove baked mushrooms from pan, discarding any remaining liquid. Serve immediately. Makes 12 to 14 servings.

Tip

When a recipe calls for shredding, use the coarse side of a hand grater to obtain larger pieces. The term "grated" indicates smaller pieces, so use the fine side of a grater.

How to Make Herbed Accordion Potatoes

Crispy Potato Skins

A popular appetizer served in many restaurants is easy to prepare at home.

4 baking potatoes
2 tablespoons butter, melted
Seasoned salt
Pepper

1 cup grated Cheddar cheese (4 oz.)
1/3 cup chopped green onions (5 to 6 onions)
6 crisp-cooked bacon slices, crumbled
1/4 cup dairy sour cream, if desired

Preheat oven to 425F (220C). Scrub and dry potatoes; prick with a fork. Bake 50 to 60 minutes or until soft; cool enough to handle. Cut each potato in half lengthwise. With a spoon or melon-baller, scoop out pulp leaving a 1/8- to 1/16-inch shell; set potato pulp aside for another use. Place potato shells, skin-side down, in a 13" x 9" baking pan. Brush inside of shells with melted butter. Sprinkle with seasoned salt and pepper. Bake 10 minutes. Remove from oven; set aside. In a small bowl, combine cheese, green onions and bacon. Using 2 forks, toss cheese mixture lightly. Spread about 2 tablespoons cheese mixture in each potato skin. Change oven setting to broil. Broil potato skins, 3 to 4 inches below heat, 1 to 1-1/2 minutes or until bubbly. Serve hot, either whole or cut in bite-size pieces. Serve with sour cream as a garnish or dip, if desired. Makes 8 potato skins or about 32 bite-size pieces.

Herbed Accordion Potatoes

A new and attractive way to prepare baked potatoes.

1/3 cup butter or margarine, melted
1 tablespoon chopped fresh chives
1 tablespoon chopped fresh parsley
1/8 teaspoon paprika
1/2 teaspoon salt

1/8 teaspoon pepper
1/4 teaspoon fines herbes
6 medium baking potatoes
1/3 cup grated Parmesan cheese (1 oz.)

Preheat oven to 425F (220C). In a small bowl, combine butter or margarine, chives, parsley, paprika, salt, pepper and fines herbes; set aside. Peel potatoes. Slice across potatoes at 1/4-inch intervals, almost to bottom. Do not slice completely through potato. Brush potatoes with butter or margarine mixture. Wrap each potato in foil; place in a shallow baking pan. Bake about 30 minutes or until nearly tender. Open and fold back foil to expose top of each potato. Sprinkle with cheese. Return to oven 10 to 15 minutes longer or until tender and light-golden color on top. Serve hot. Makes 6 servings.

Blue-Ribbon Creamy Potatoes

Shred cooked potatoes to give a special texture not possible with mashed potatoes.

7 to 8 medium potatoes
1/4 cup butter or margarine,
   room temperature
1/2 cup dairy sour cream
1 (10-1/2-oz.) can condensed
   cream of chicken soup

1/4 cup minced green onions
1 teaspoon salt
1/4 teaspoon pepper
2 cups shredded Cheddar cheese (8 oz.)

Boil or bake unpeeled potatoes until nearly tender. Peel potatoes; shred on wide part of a hand grater. Preheat oven to 350F (175C). In a large bowl, combine shredded potatoes, butter or margarine, sour cream, condensed soup, green onions, salt, pepper and half the cheese. Spoon potato mixture into a 1-1/2-quart baking dish. Sprinkle top with remaining cheese. Bake 30 minutes or until cheese is bubbly. Serve hot. Makes 6 servings.

Cosmopolitan Potatoes

Up-town version of the time-honored scalloped potatoes.

6 medium potatoes, peeled, thinly sliced
1/2 teaspoon salt
1/8 teaspoon pepper
1/4 cup butter, melted

1/8 teaspoon ground nutmeg
1 tablespoon chopped fresh parsley
2 cups shredded Monterey Jack cheese (8 oz.)
1 cup chicken stock or bouillon

Preheat oven to 375F (190C). In a large bowl, toss potatoes with salt, pepper, butter, nutmeg and parsley. Arrange half the potato mixture in a 1-1/2-quart baking dish. Sprinkle half the cheese over potato mixture. Repeat with remaining potato mixture and cheese. Pour stock or bouillon over all. Bake, uncovered, 50 to 55 minutes or until tender. Serve hot. Makes 4 to 6 servings.

Curried Sweet-Potato Soup

Don't overlook the possibility of serving this soup cold; it's great either way!

2 medium sweet potatoes, about 1-1/2 lbs.
1-1/2 teaspoons salt
1/4 cup flaked coconut
1/2 cup milk
1 cup chicken stock or bouillon

1/4 cup chutney, fruit pieces and juice
1 teaspoon curry powder
1 tablespoon lemon juice
1 cup half and half
1/3 cup chopped peanuts

Peel sweet potatoes; cut in chunks. Place potato chunks in a medium saucepan. Add salt and cover with water. Cook potatoes, over medium heat, 10 to 15 minutes or until soft; drain and set aside. In a small saucepan, combine coconut and milk. Cook over very low heat until hot, but do not boil. In a blender or food processor, combine coconut mixture, stock or bouillon, chutney, curry powder and lemon juice; process until smooth. Add cooked potatoes; process until pureed. Pour pureed mixture into medium saucepan, add half and half. Heat to desired serving temperature. Ladle into individual soup bowls. Sprinkle chopped peanuts over soup. Serve immediately. Makes 4 to 5 servings.

Banana-Squash Sauté

A quick and easy way to serve squash.

1-1/2 lbs. banana squash
1/4 cup butter or margarine
2 tablespoons vegetable oil

1/4 cup slivered almonds
1/4 teaspoon ground cinnamon
1 tablespoon honey

Peel squash; cut in pieces about 3 inches long and 1/2 inch wide. In a large skillet, heat butter or margarine and oil. Sauté squash pieces over medium heat until golden brown on 1 side. Turn and sauté other side until tender. Remove squash from pan; keep warm. Add almonds, cinnamon and honey to skillet. Cook over medium heat until almonds are golden. Spoon almond mixture over cooked squash. Serve warm. Makes 5 to 6 servings.

Herbed Zucchini

Whenever fresh oregano and basil are available, substitute them for the dried ones.

2 tablespoons vegetable oil
4 medium zucchini, cut in 1/8-inch slices
1 onion, sliced
1/2 teaspoon salt
1/8 teaspoon pepper
1/4 teaspoon dried leaf oregano

1/4 teaspoon dried leaf basil
4 oz. sliced Monterey Jack cheese
3 tomatoes, sliced
1/2 cup soft breadcrumbs
2 tablespoons butter or margarine, melted
2 tablespoons grated Parmesan cheese

Preheat oven to 350F (175C). Heat oil in a medium skillet; add zucchini and onion. Sauté in oil until nearly tender; drain. Stir in salt, pepper, oregano and basil. In a 10'' x 6'' shallow baking dish, arrange alternate layers of cooked zucchini mixture, Monterey Jack cheese and sliced tomatoes. In a small bowl, combine breadcrumbs, butter or margarine and Parmesan cheese. Sprinkle crumb mixture over tomatoes. Bake 25 to 30 minutes. Serve hot. Makes 5 to 6 servings.

Upside-Down Zucchini Pie

Uncooked filling will not quite fill pan, but will expand when baked.

4 medium zucchini
2 tablespoons vegetable oil
2 eggs
1 cup cottage cheese (8 oz.)
1/4 cup butter or margarine,
    room temperature
1/4 cup all-purpose flour

1/2 teaspoon baking powder
1/4 teaspoon salt
1 cup dairy sour cream
1/4 cup grated Parmesan cheese (3/4 oz.)
1 tomato, peeled, thinly sliced
Parsley sprigs for garnish

Cut zucchini crosswise in 1/4-inch slices. Heat oil in a large skillet. Add zucchini; sauté until softened but not mushy. Line bottom and side of a 9-inch pie plate with sautéed zucchini slices; set aside. Preheat oven to 350F (175C). In a large bowl, beat eggs. Beat in cottage cheese and butter or margarine until nearly smooth. Stir in flour, baking powder and salt until blended. Stir in sour cream and cheese until distributed. Pour mixture into zucchini-lined pie plate; smooth top gently with a spatula. Carefully arrange tomato slices over top of filling. Bake 35 to 45 minutes or until firm in center. Cool on a rack 10 minutes. Invert on a 12-inch round platter. Garnish center with parsley sprigs. Cut in wedges. Serve warm. Makes 5 to 6 servings.

Italian-Style Zucchini

To make ahead, prepare and refrigerate mixture in baking dish; heat at serving time.

2 lbs. zucchini, diced (about 7 medium)
2 tablespoons chopped onion
1 cup water
1/2 teaspoon salt
1/8 teaspoon dried Italian herbs

1 egg, slightly beaten
1/2 cup grated Parmesan cheese (1-1/2 oz.)
2 tablespoons butter or margarine, melted
1/2 cup soft breadcrumbs

Preheat oven to 350F (175C). Butter a 1-quart baking dish. In a large saucepan, combine zucchini, onion, water, salt and herbs. Cover and simmer 10 to 15 minutes or until zucchini is tender; drain well. Mash zucchini; stir in egg and cheese. Spoon zucchini mixture into buttered baking dish. In a small bowl, combine melted butter or margarine and breadcrumbs. Sprinkle crumb mixture over zucchini mixture. Bake 30 minutes or until topping is golden brown. Serve hot. Makes 5 to 6 servings.

Glazed Squash Rings

Quick to fix with super flavor.

2 acorn squash
1/2 cup maple-flavored syrup
1/8 teaspoon ground allspice

1/2 cup apple juice
1/4 cup butter or margarine, melted

Cut each squash crosswise in 1-inch-thick rings. Remove seeds but do not peel. Place in a large skillet. In a small bowl, combine maple-flavored syrup, allspice, apple juice and butter or margarine. Pour syrup mixture over squash. Cover and simmer 12 to 15 minutes or until squash is nearly tender. Uncover; spoon sauce over each slice. Simmer 5 minutes longer. Serve hot. Makes 5 to 6 servings.

Golden-Strand Squash

A dazzling show-stopper—perfect with roast pork or chicken.

1 (2-1/2- to 3-lb.) spaghetti squash
1/2 cup butter or margarine,
  room temperature
2 tablespoons brown sugar

1/4 teaspoon ground cinnamon
1/4 teaspoon salt
1/4 cup chopped pistachios or walnuts
1 orange, peeled, chopped

Preheat oven to 375F (190C). Cut squash in half lengthwise. Using a spoon, scrape out seeds and loose stringy portion. Place squash halves, cut-side down, on a shallow baking pan. Bake 35 to 45 minutes or until tender. While baking squash, combine in a small bowl, butter or margarine, brown sugar, cinnamon, salt and nuts. Invert baked squash shells. Using a fork, pull spaghetti-like strands up. Add half the nut mixture to each cooked-squash half. Lightly toss with fork. Top with orange pieces. Serve warm. Makes 6 to 8 servings.

Squash Supreme

Summer squash at its best.

8 crookneck squash, cut in 1-inch cubes
1 medium onion, chopped
1/4 cup butter or margarine
2 eggs, beaten
3/4 cup soft breadcrumbs

1/8 teaspoon ground nutmeg
1/2 teaspoon salt
1/8 teaspoon pepper
2 tablespoons butter or margarine, melted
1/2 cup soft breadcrumbs

Grease a 1-1/2-quart baking dish; set aside. In a large saucepan, cook squash and onion in about 1 inch of water 15 minutes or until very tender; drain. Preheat oven to 350F (175C). Process cooked squash in a blender or food processor with 1/4 cup butter or margarine until nearly smooth. Add eggs, 3/4 cup breadcrumbs, nutmeg, salt and pepper; process until mixed. Pour squash mixture into greased baking dish. In a small bowl or measuring cup, combine 2 tablespoons melted butter or margarine with 1/2 cup breadcrumbs. Sprinkle crumb mixture over casserole. Bake 45 to 50 minutes or until center is firm but not dry. Serve hot. Makes 6 to 8 servings.

Squash Medley with Herbs

This dish is a colorful combination of yellow and green.

2 crookneck squash
2 medium zucchini
1 teaspoon salt
1/4 cup butter or margarine

1/4 teaspoon dried leaf basil
1 tablespoon chopped fresh chives
1 tablespoon chopped fresh parsley
1/4 teaspoon dried leaf marjoram

Shred unpeeled crookneck squash and zucchini on large side of a hand grater or in a food processor. Sprinkle shredded squash with salt; toss to mix. Place salted squash in a colander over a pie plate. Let stand to drain 1/2 hour; squeeze out excess water. In a medium skillet, melt butter or margarine. Add shredded squash. Sauté, uncovered, 5 to 6 minutes or until nearly tender. Stir in basil, chives, parsley and marjoram. Cover and cook 1 minute. Serve hot. Makes 4 servings.

How to Make Fennel-Tomato Bake

1/Trim fennel tops, leaving about 1 inch above bulb. Cut fennel in half lengthwise.

2/Sprinkle seasoned bread cubes over fennel mixture. Bake until golden brown.

Fennel-Tomato Bake

Other names for fennel are finocchio and sweet anise.

3 fennel bulbs
1/4 cup olive oil or vegetable oil
1 garlic clove, crushed
2 fresh tomatoes, peeled, seeded, chopped
1/2 teaspoon salt

1/8 teaspoon pepper
2 slices bread
1/4 cup butter, melted
1/4 cup grated Parmesan cheese (3/4 oz.)

Preheat oven to 375F (190C). Trim fennel tops, leaving about 1 inch above bulb. Cut fennel in half lengthwise. Cut in 1/8-inch-thick slices. Heat oil in a large skillet. Add fennel slices and garlic; sauté until nearly tender. Stir in tomatoes, salt and pepper; cook 2 to 3 minutes. Spoon fennel mixture into a 2-quart shallow baking dish. Remove crust from bread. Cut in small cubes, about the size of small croutons. In a small bowl, toss together soft bread cubes, butter and cheese. Sprinkle seasoned bread cubes over fennel mixture. Bake 10 to 15 minutes or until topping is golden. Serve hot. Makes 5 to 6 servings.

Tip

When a recipe calls for soft breadcrumbs, it means crumbs you make from fresh bread by pulling it apart with your fingers or by quickly pulverizing it in a blender or food processor. Dry breadcrumbs are made of finely crushed dry bread. Breadcrumbs are available in plain or seasoned flavors on grocery shelves or can be made at home from dry bread.

Sweet-Sour Baked Tomatoes

If juice oozes from tomatoes while baking, spoon it over tomatoes before adding topping.

3 large tomatoes
1/4 cup lightly packed brown sugar
3 bacon slices, finely chopped
1 small onion, finely chopped

1 teaspoon cornstarch
1/4 teaspoon salt
1/8 teaspoon pepper
1/2 cup dairy sour cream

Preheat oven to 350F (175C). Cut tomatoes in halves crosswise; place, cut-side up, in a shallow 11" x 7" baking pan. Bake tomatoes 12 minutes. Sprinkle brown sugar on cut surfaces of tomatoes; bake 5 minutes longer. In a small skillet, cook bacon and onion until bacon is crisp. Add cornstarch, salt and pepper. Cook, stirring 1 minute. Stir in sour cream. Cook until heated, but not boiling. Spoon bacon mixture over baked tomato halves. Serve hot. Makes 6 servings.

Garden-Fresh Ratatouille

A practical dish when vegetables are plentiful and reasonably priced.

1/4 cup vegetable oil
1 small onion, diced
1 garlic clove, crushed
1 small unpeeled eggplant,
   cut in 1/2-inch cubes
2 small zucchini, cut crosswise in
   1/2-inch slices
2 celery stalks, cut crosswise in
   1/2-inch slices
1 small green bell pepper, cut in
   1/2-inch squares

2 small tomatoes, peeled, seeded,
   cut in wedges
1/4 lb. mushrooms, cut in quarters
1 tablespoon chopped fresh parsley
1 teaspoon salt
1/4 teaspoon pepper
1/2 teaspoon dried leaf basil
1/2 teaspoon dried leaf oregano

Pour oil in a large skillet; add onion and garlic. Sauté 2 to 3 minutes. Add eggplant, zucchini and celery; cover and cook 10 minutes, stirring occasionally. Stir in green pepper, tomatoes, mushrooms, parsley, salt, pepper, basil and oregano. Simmer, uncovered, 6 to 8 minutes or until vegetables are tender. Serve hot. Makes about 8 servings.

Fiesta Rice

A well-seasoned accompaniment for a roast.

1/4 cup butter or margarine
1 cup uncooked white rice
1 celery stalk, chopped
1 fresh or canned whole green chili,
   seeded, chopped

1 tablespoon chopped green onion
1 medium tomato, peeled, seeded, chopped
1 teaspoon salt
2 cups chicken stock or bouillon

Melt butter or margarine in a large skillet. Add rice; sauté until rice begins to turn golden in color. Stir in celery, green chili, green onion, tomato, salt and stock or bouillon. Cover and simmer 25 to 30 minutes or until rice is tender. Serve hot. Makes 5 to 6 servings.

Golden Grove Rice

Wonderful to serve with chicken.

1/4 cup butter or margarine
1 cup uncooked white rice
1 small onion, chopped
1/2 cup chopped celery
1 cup chicken stock or bouillon

1-1/2 cups orange juice
1 teaspoon grated orange peel
1 teaspoon salt
1/2 cup raisins or golden raisins
1/4 cup toasted slivered almonds

In a large skillet, combine butter or margarine, rice and onion. Sauté until rice is a light-golden color. Add celery, stock or bouillon, orange juice, orange peel, salt and raisins. Cover and simmer 25 to 30 minutes or until rice is tender. Sprinkle almonds over the top. Serve hot. Makes 4 to 5 servings.

Chili-Rice Bake

If you're pressed for time, make ahead and heat at serving time.

3 cups cooked white rice
1 (4-oz.) can diced green chilies, drained

1 cup dairy sour cream
2 cups shredded Cheddar cheese (8 oz.)

Preheat oven to 350F (175C). Butter a 1-1/2- or 2-quart baking dish. Spread half the rice evenly in baking dish. Top with half the green chilies; then half the sour cream and cheese. Repeat, ending with cheese. Bake 20 to 30 minutes or until cheese melts. Serve hot. Makes 5 to 6 servings.

Garden-Fresh Stir-Fry

Carrots are cooked first because they take longer to cook than other vegetables.

2 tablespoons vegetable oil
1 garlic clove, crushed
1 teaspoon finely chopped gingerroot or
   1/4 teaspoon ground ginger
2 carrots, cut in 1/8-inch-thick circles
2 cups julienned fresh green beans
2 cups thinly sliced cauliflowerets

2 tablespoons water
1 tablespoon lemon juice
1/4 teaspoon salt
1/8 teaspoon pepper
2 teaspoons cornstarch
3 tablespoons soy sauce
1/4 cup sliced toasted almonds

In a large skillet or wok, heat oil. Add garlic, ginger and carrots. Cook, stirring constantly, over high heat 2 minutes. Add beans and cauliflower. Cook, stirring 1 minute longer. Add water, lemon juice, salt and pepper. Cover and cook 2 to 3 minutes or until vegetables are nearly tender. In a small bowl, dissolve cornstarch in soy sauce; stir into vegetable mixture. Cook, stirring, 1 minute. Sprinkle with almonds. Serve immediately. Makes 5 to 6 servings.

Meats & Accompaniments

O ur main dishes are as varied as the heritage of people who live in California. Many have flavors from South of the border. Others use ingredients that are popular in Oriental or Italian cooking. And still others are homey with a typical American style. All are designed to taste good and be easy on your budget. In fact, we extend meats with ingredients such as vegetables, cheese or tortillas.

BUDGET-EXTENDERS

You can't reduce meat prices, but you can make the most of what you buy. First, read food ads in your local paper and plan menus around a week's best buys. Learn more about meat cuts and proper meat cookery. Ask your butcher questions and carefully read labels for exact names of various meats. Refrigerate or freeze meat promptly when you get home to make sure it stays fresh. Use your freezer to help economize. When a cut of meat is on sale, buy two or more. Freeze extra ones for later use.

Also, take advantage of seasonal peaks in abundance and quality. This applies to meats and vegetables or fruits used with them. Ranchero Bake is less costly when zucchini and tomatoes are at peak season.

Traditionally, less-tender cuts of meats, requiring long slow cooking, are more economical. One-pot cooking is a great way to save time and fuel. Fruited Pot Roast is an example of this type of food. It glamorizes an economical cut of meat by the addition of spices and California's dried fruits. Lift the lid while it's cooking and tantalizing aromas will fill your kitchen. Pinto beans and tomatoes are used to extend stew beef in our Family-Style Chili & Beans.

TIME-SAVERS

We realize that today's active consumer doesn't have time for lengthy cooking after getting home from work or after a busy day on community projects. Children are hungry or often dinner must be rushed to make an evening class or meeting. For those situations, try Mexican Skillet Dinner. It's a quick-and-easy main dish featuring items that are likely to be on your pantry shelves or in the refrigerator. No-Fuss Tostadas are easy to put together, too. Do all the chopping and shredding before you leave for work. Keep each item in a separate plastic bag in the refrigerator. While the taco-seasoning mix is simmering, fry the tortillas. You'll be ready to assemble everything within a few minutes after arriving home.❖

Mexican-Style Lasagne

Tortillas and enchilada sauce replace traditional lasagne noodles and Italian sauce.

1 lb. lean ground beef	1/4 cup vegetable oil
1 onion, chopped	8 (6-inch) corn tortillas
1/2 cup chopped celery	8 oz. Monterey Jack cheese, thinly sliced
1 garlic clove, crushed	1 cup ricotta cheese (8 oz.)
1 (16-oz.) can tomatoes, chopped	1 egg, beaten
1 (11-oz.) can or jar enchilada sauce	1 cup shredded Cheddar cheese (4 oz.)
1 teaspoon salt	

In a large skillet, combine beef, onion, celery and garlic. Cook until beef is browned. Add tomatoes, enchilada sauce and salt. Cook uncovered, 15 minutes, stirring occasionally. Heat oil in a medium skillet. Add 1 tortilla; cook over medium heat until tortilla is soft but not crisp. Drain on paper towel. Repeat with remaining tortillas. Cut each tortilla in half. Preheat oven to 350F (175C). Spread 1/3 meat mixture on bottom of a 13" x 9" baking pan. Top with 1/2 the Monterey Jack cheese. In a small bowl, combine ricotta cheese and egg. Spread 1/2 the ricotta-cheese mixture over Monterey Jack cheese. Add a layer of 1/2 the softened tortillas. Repeat layering, ending with 1/3 of meat sauce on top. Sprinkle with Cheddar cheese. Bake 20 to 25 minutes or until cheese melts and mixture is bubbly. Makes 6 to 8 servings.

No-Fuss Tostadas

To top the tostadas, offer a choice of taco sauce or Russian salad dressing.

1 lb. lean ground beef	1-1/2 cups shredded Cheddar or
1 (1-1/4-oz.) pkg. taco-seasoning mix	Monterey Jack cheese (6 oz.)
1 cup water	2 large tomatoes, chopped
1 (16-oz.) can refried beans	3 green onions, finely chopped
1/2 cup vegetable oil	1/2 cup dairy sour cream
5 or 6 flour or corn tortillas	1 avocado
1 small head iceberg lettuce, shredded	

In a medium skillet, brown ground beef, stirring until crumbly; drain off fat. Add taco mix and water. Simmer, uncovered, 10 minutes. In a small saucepan, heat beans. In medium skillet, heat oil over medium heat. Fry 1 tortilla in hot oil until crisp, turning as necessary; drain on paper towel. Repeat for remaining tortillas. Spread warm beans on crisp tortilla. Top each tortilla with browned ground beef, lettuce, cheese, tomatoes and green onions. Garnish top with sour cream. Peel and thinly slice avocado. Arrange avocado slices around edge of each tostada. Serve immediately. Makes 5 or 6 servings.

Busy-Day Tacos

Good way to make tacos if you're a novice or in a hurry.

1 lb. lean ground beef
1 (1-1/4-oz.) pkg. taco-seasoning mix
3/4 cup water
3/4 cup vegetable oil
12 (6-inch) corn tortillas

3 cups shredded lettuce
2 large tomatoes, chopped
1 cup shredded Cheddar cheese (4 oz.)
1/2 cup dairy sour cream, if desired
1 large avocado, thinly sliced, if desired

In a large skillet, brown ground beef until crumbly; drain off any fat. Stir in seasoning mix and water. Simmer uncovered, 15 minutes, stirring occasionally. In another large skillet, heat oil to 350F (175C). Fry 1 tortilla until it becomes soft; then fold it in half and hold slightly open in a U-shape with tongs. Fry until crisp and light brown; drain on paper towel. Keep warm on a baking sheet in a 200F (95C) oven. Fry remaining tortillas. Fill each fried tortilla shell with meat mixture. Top with lettuce, tomatoes and cheese. Top with sour cream and avocado, if desired. Serve immediately. Makes 6 servings.

Mexican Skillet Dinner

A quick and easy main dish, thanks to convenience foods from your pantry shelf.

1 lb. lean ground beef
1 small onion, chopped
1 (8-oz.) can tomatoes
1/4 cup chopped green bell pepper
1 (16-oz.) can cream-style corn
1/4 cup sliced pitted ripe olives

1/2 teaspoon salt
1/8 teaspoon pepper
1 garlic clove, crushed
1 (15-oz.) can tamales, cut in 1-inch pieces
1 cup shredded Cheddar cheese (4 oz.)

In a 10-inch skillet, brown beef with onion over medium heat. Chop tomatoes, reserving liquid. To beef mixture, add chopped tomatoes and liquid, green pepper, corn, olives, salt, pepper and garlic. Stir to combine. Carefully stir in tamales. Cover beef mixture and simmer 15 minutes. Sprinkle cheese over beef mixture. Cover and let stand 2 to 3 minutes or until cheese melts. Serve hot. Makes 6 servings.

Ranchero Bake

A complete meal in one casserole.

1 lb. lean ground beef
1 small onion chopped
2 zucchini, diced
1 tomato, diced
1 (4-oz.) can diced green chilies, drained

1 teaspoon salt
1 garlic clove, crushed
2 cups cooked white rice
1 cup dairy sour cream
2 cups shredded Cheddar cheese (8 oz.)

Preheat oven to 350F (175C). In a 10-inch skillet, lightly brown beef. Add onion and zucchini. Cook over medium heat until vegetables are nearly tender. Stir in tomato, green chilies, salt and garlic. Heat through. Spoon rice into a 2-quart baking dish. Spoon beef mixture over rice. Top with sour cream. Sprinkle cheese over sour cream. Bake 20 to 30 minutes or until mixture bubbles. Serve hot. Makes about 6 servings.

Family-Style Chili & Beans

For real chili fans, add more chili powder to this mild, yet flavorful stew.

1/4 cup all-purpose flour	1 (8-oz.) can stewed tomatoes with juice
1/2 teaspoon salt	1 teaspoon brown sugar
1/8 teaspoon pepper	1/2 teaspoon dry mustard
1 lb. beef for stew, cut in 1/2-inch cubes	1 teaspoon chili powder
2 tablespoons vegetable oil	1 (15-oz.) can pinto beans, drained
1 small onion, chopped	1/2 cup shredded sharp Cheddar cheese
1 cup beef stock or bouillon	(2 oz.)

In a small bowl, combine flour, salt and pepper. Coat beef cubes with flour mixture. Heat oil in a 10-inch skillet over medium heat. Add beef; brown on all sides in hot oil. Add onion, stock or bouillon, tomatoes, brown sugar, mustard and chili powder. Cover and simmer 1-1/2 hours or until beef is tender. Add beans; bring to a boil. Spoon chili into 4 or 5 individual soup bowls. Sprinkle cheese over chili. Serve hot. Makes 4 to 5 servings.

Spicy Shredded-Beef Sandwiches

Use half of a large French roll or a whole small French roll for each serving.

1 to 1-1/2 lbs. beef for stew or	1 tablespoon brown sugar
boneless beef chuck roast	1 teaspoon Worcestershire sauce
2 tablespoons vegetable oil	1/2 teaspoon dry mustard
1 onion, chopped	1/2 teaspoon chili powder
1 cup beef stock or bouillon	1/2 teaspoon salt
1/3 cup Burgundy	2 (7-inch) or 4 (3-inch) French rolls
1/4 cup chili sauce	

Cut beef in 1-inch cubes. Heat oil in a large pan or Dutch oven over medium heat. Add beef; brown on all sides in hot oil. Add onion, stock or bouillon, Burgundy, chili sauce, brown sugar, Worcestershire sauce, dry mustard, chili powder and salt. Cover and simmer 2 hours or until beef is tender. Using 2 forks, shred beef. Cut rolls in halves horizontally. Toast cut surfaces. Spoon beef and sauce on cut-side of rolls. Serve warm, open-face-style. Makes 4 servings.

Sierra Beef Jerky

Partially freezing meat will make it easier to slice.

1 (1-1/2-lb.) beef flank steak	1/4 teaspoon garlic salt
1/4 cup soy sauce	

Trim any fat from beef; slice beef in 1/4-inch-thick strips. Slice beef with the grain for a chewy jerky; or, slice across the grain for a more tender jerky. Brush both sides of strips with soy sauce; sprinkle with garlic salt. Arrange a single layer of beef strips in 2 (15" x 10") shallow baking pans. Set oven at 185F (85C). Cook beef 3 hours. Turn strips; cook 2 to 3 hours longer or until dry. Makes about 35 strips.

How to Make Party Pita

1/Shred beef by pulling small pieces apart with 2 forks.

2/Spoon beef and cabbage mixtures into each bread.

Party Pita

Prepare fillings ahead of time for a quick after-the-game party.

1-1/2 to 2 lbs. beef for stew,
   cut in 1-inch cubes
1/4 cup all-purpose flour
2 tablespoons vegetable oil
1/2 cup dry red wine
1 bay leaf
1/2 teaspoon salt
4 whole peppercorns
4 whole cloves
1 cup beef stock or bouillon

2 tablespoons brown sugar
1 onion, finely chopped
2 carrots, shredded
3 cups shredded red or green cabbage
1/2 cup plain yogurt
1/2 teaspoon seasoned salt
1/2 teaspoon prepared mustard
1 teaspoon honey
8 pita bread rounds
Ripe olives for garnish

Coat beef cubes with flour. Heat oil in a 10-inch skillet over medium heat. Add beef; brown on all sides in hot oil. Set beef aside. In a small saucepan, combine wine, bay leaf, salt, peppercorns, cloves, stock or bouillon and brown sugar. Bring to a boil; simmer 5 minutes. Strain mixture, discarding spices. Pour liquid over browned beef cubes. Add onion and carrots. Cover and simmer 1-1/2 hours or until beef is tender. Shred beef by pulling small pieces apart with 2 forks; set aside. In a small bowl, combine cabbage, yogurt, seasoned salt, mustard and honey. Cut each pita bread open. Spoon about 1/3 cup beef mixture into each pita bread. Top meat mixture with 1/4 cup cabbage mixture. Garnish with ripe olives. Serve warm. Makes 8 servings.

Fruited Pot Roast

An economical cut of beef, glamorized with spices and fruit.

2 tablespoons vegetable oil
1 (3- to 4-lb.) beef chuck 7-bone pot roast
1 small onion, sliced
1 carrot, chopped
2 teaspoons salt
1/4 teaspoon pepper
1 qt. (4 cups) beef stock or bouillon

1/8 teaspoon ground allspice
1/8 teaspoon ground ginger
1/2 cup pitted prunes
1/2 cup dried peaches or apricots
1/4 cup all-purpose flour
1/2 cup cold water

Heat oil in a large heavy saucepan or Dutch oven over medium heat. Add pot roast; brown on all sides in hot oil. Add onion, carrot, salt, pepper, stock or bouillon, allspice and ginger. Cover and simmer 2 hours or until nearly tender. Add prunes and peaches or apricots. Cover and cook 20 minutes longer. Remove beef and fruit to a platter; keep warm. In a small bowl, combine flour and water; stir mixture into meat juices. Bring to a boil; simmer 3 minutes, stirring constantly. Serve gravy with beef. Makes 6 servings.

Picnic Ham Loaf

A welcome entree on a hot summer day.

1 (8-oz.) can sliced pineapple
3 cups diced cooked ham (about 1 lb.)
2 eggs
1/4 cup milk
1 cup cornflake cereal, crushed

1 teaspoon prepared mustard
1/2 teaspoon prepared horseradish
1/2 teaspoon salt
1/8 teaspoon pepper
1 lb. lean ground beef

Drain pineapple, reserving juice. Arrange pineapple slices on bottom of a 9" x 5" loaf pan; set aside. Grind ham in a meat grinder or with the metal blade of food processor; set aside. In a large bowl, combine pineapple juice and eggs. Add milk, cornflake crumbs, mustard, horseradish, salt and pepper. Add ground ham and ground beef to egg mixture; mix thoroughly. Press meat mixture in pan over pineapple slices. Place in a cold oven. Set oven at 350F (175C). Bake ham loaf 1-1/4 hours. Remove from oven; let stand in pan 15 minutes. Invert ham loaf on a platter. Cover and refrigerate at least 2 hours. Slice and serve cold. Makes 6 to 8 servings.

Behind-The-Scenes Food Tour

To enjoy spectacular California landscaping, plus a behind-the-scenes view of food products, visit the corporate headquarters of Lawry's Foods in Los Angeles. Short tours of Lawry's California Center include production facilities, laboratories and test kitchens for such products as seasoned salt, salad dressings and seasoning-mixes. In addition, at certain times of the year, lunches and dinners are served featuring typical California foods in a garden setting. It's a perfect place to include on your California tour.

How to Make Zucchini Lasagne

1/Cut cooked zucchini in 1/4-inch-thick lengthwise slices.

2/Layer zucchini, egg mixture, cheese slices and meat sauce in baking dish.

Zucchini Lasagne

So good to eat and good for you.

4 medium zucchini, unpeeled	1/4 teaspoon pepper
1 lb. lean ground beef	1/2 teaspoon dried leaf oregano
1 onion, chopped	1 tablespoon chopped fresh parsley
2 (8-oz.) cans tomato sauce	1 egg
1 (6-oz.) can tomato paste	2 cups cottage cheese (1 lb.)
1/2 cup water	8 oz. sliced mozzarella cheese
1 teaspoon salt	1/2 cup grated Parmesan cheese (1-1/2 oz.)

Steam or boil whole zucchini until barely tender, about 10 minutes. Drain zucchini; cut in 1/4-inch-thick lengthwise slices and set aside. In a large skillet, sauté beef and onion until browned. Add tomato sauce, tomato paste, water, salt, pepper, oregano and parsley. Simmer, covered, 35 minutes. Preheat oven to 350F (175C). In a small bowl, combine egg and cottage cheese; set aside. Spread a small amount of meat sauce over bottom of a 13'' x 9'' baking dish. Arrange 1/3 sliced cooked zucchini over bottom of baking dish. Add 1/3 each of egg mixture, mozzarella-cheese slices and remaining meat sauce. Repeat layering twice. Sprinkle top with grated Parmesan cheese. Bake 40 to 45 minutes or until bubbly. Serve hot. Makes 6 to 8 servings.

Sunny California Chops

Orange slices and a wine sauce flavor and moisten these chops.

6 (1-inch-thick) pork loin or rib chops
Salt and pepper
1 onion, cut in 6 slices
2 oranges, peeled
3 dried figs, cut in halves

1/3 cup dry white wine
2 tablespoons honey
1/8 teaspoon ground cinnamon
1 teaspoon finely chopped
 crystallized ginger

Place chops in a broiler pan; season with salt and pepper. Top each chop with an onion slice. Cut each orange in 3 thick slices; place 1 orange slice on each onion slice. Top each orange slice with a fig half. Preheat oven to 350F (175C). In small bowl, combine wine, honey, cinnamon and ginger. Pour mixture over chops; cover with foil. Bake 40 minutes. Uncover and bake 10 to 15 minutes longer or until pork is tender. Serve chops with hot sauce. Makes 6 servings.

Plum-Glazed Chops

For a change, try this do-it-yourself plum sauce with chicken.

1 (16-3/4-oz.) can whole purple plums
1 garlic clove, chopped
1 tablespoon lemon juice
2 tablespoons soy sauce

2 tablespoons brown sugar
1 tablespoon chopped crystallized ginger
6 (1/2-inch-thick) pork chops
Salt and pepper

Preheat oven to 350F (175C). Drain plums, reserving 1/2 cup juice. Remove pits from plums. In a blender or food processor, puree drained plums, reserved juice, garlic, lemon juice, soy sauce, brown sugar and ginger. Pour pureed plum mixture in a small saucepan. Bring to a boil. Reduce heat and simmer, uncovered, 5 minutes; set aside. Season chops with salt and pepper. Arrange chops in a 13" x 9" baking pan. Bake chops 20 minutes. Turn chops; pour plum sauce over chops. Bake 20 minutes longer or until pork is tender. Serve hot. Makes 6 servings.

Oven-Baked Barbecued Spareribs

Precook ribs in water; then bake with sauce for succulent tender meat.

3 to 4 lbs. fresh pork spareribs
Salt
Pepper
1/4 cup molasses
2 tablespoons prepared mustard

1 tablespoon vinegar
1 teaspoon chili powder
1 tablespoon Worcestershire sauce
1/2 cup ketchup
1 tablespoon minced green onion

Place spareribs in a Dutch oven or large pan; cover with water. Bring to a boil; simmer 30 minutes and drain. Preheat oven to 375F (190C). Arrange spareribs on a 15" x 10" shallow baking pan; season ribs with salt and pepper. In a small bowl, combine molasses, mustard, vinegar, chili powder, Worcestershire sauce, ketchup and green onion. Brush spareribs with molasses mixture. Bake 15 minutes; turn spareribs and brush with sauce. Bake 15 to 20 minutes longer. Serve hot or cold. Makes 4 to 5 servings.

California Peach Chutney

Keep on hand to serve with curried chicken or pork.

5 medium peaches, peeled, sliced
1/2 cup chopped dates
1/2 cup chopped dried figs
1/4 cup finely chopped crystallized ginger
1 small onion, chopped
1 cup lightly packed brown sugar

1 cup cider vinegar
1 teaspoon salt
1/2 teaspoon ground nutmeg
1/2 teaspoon ground allspice
1/8 teaspoon dried red-pepper flakes

Combine all ingredients in a 3-quart saucepan. Bring to a boil. Simmer, stirring frequently, 30 minutes or until thickened. Wash 5 (1/2-pint) jars in hot soapy water; rinse. Keep hot until needed. Prepare self-sealing lids as manufacturer directs. Ladle hot chutney into 1 hot jar at a time, leaving 1/4-inch headspace. Release trapped air. Wipe rim of jar with a clean damp cloth. Attach self-sealing lid. Repeat with remaining jars. Place filled jars on a rack in a large pot of boiling water. Water should cover jars 1 to 2 inches and have an additional 2 inches for boiling space. Cover pot. Bring water to a boil. At sea level, boil 10 minutes. For every 1000 feet altitude, add 1 minute to boiling time. Store up to 1 year. Makes 4 to 5 (1/2 pints).

Zucchini-Corn Relish

A great relish with barbecued chicken or ribs.

2 large zucchini, coarsely shredded
1 cup cooked fresh or frozen corn
1/2 cup cider vinegar
2 tablespoons vegetable oil

1 tablespoon sugar
1/2 teaspoon salt
1/4 teaspoon celery seed

In a medium bowl, combine all ingredients. Cover and refrigerate 2 hours or more before serving. Makes about 3 cups.

California Pepper Relish

Cover relish and keep in refrigerator for serving with grilled meats.

3 large tomatoes, peeled, seeded, chopped
1 onion, chopped
1 green bell pepper, seeded, chopped
2 fresh whole green chilies, seeded, chopped
2 celery stalks, chopped
1 teaspoon salt

1/2 teaspoon ground ginger
1/2 teaspoon ground cinnamon
1/8 teaspoon ground cloves
1/2 cup cider vinegar
1/4 cup lightly packed brown sugar

In a large saucepan, combine all ingredients. Cook, uncovered, over medium heat 50 minutes, stirring occasionally. Cool and serve immediately or cover and refrigerate for future use. Makes 3-1/2 to 4 cups.

Outdoor Cookery

I t has been said that Californians eat everywhere. Perhaps nothing typifies that statement more than seeing a hang-glider pilot munching on a sandwich while riding the coastal up-drafts at Torrey Pines. In addition to their favorite spot—the backyard patio—they also cook and eat in parks, on the beach, onboard boats, in sports-stadium parking lots, at ski resorts and at desert off-road rallies. In fact, Californians eat in almost any conceivable spot.

Though Californians may have popularized outdoor cooking, they no longer have a monopoly on that enjoyable pastime. Barbecuing has spread across the country and the portable barbecue grill is the outdoor-cook's best friend, whether in Peoria or Pasadena.

HEAT INTENSITY

Perhaps the successful outdoor chef's single most important attribute is the ability to manage or regulate heat intensity. There is nothing more frustrating than serving guests overdone, black-charred food, or conversely, having them wait for food that is being slow-cooked by a retarded fire.

Managing heat intensity is relatively simple when using a gas-fueled or electric barbecue grill. With charcoal, heat management is more complex. First, use the minimum amount of charcoal to do the job reasonably. Build the fire in an ash-free firebox. Building a new fire on an accumulation of ashes inhibits combustion and reduces the fire's effectiveness. Positioning the food closer to or farther from the heat alters the fire's intensity on the food. If your barbecue is equipped with dampers, opening and closing them will increase and decrease heat intensity. Tapping the firebox to remove the ash coating on charcoal increases heat intensity. Allowing the ash coating to remain has the opposite effect.

GRILLING EQUIPMENT

Several pieces of basic grilling equipment will make your job easier: a metal drip pan to catch meat juices and prevent flare-ups, tongs for handling hot coals, other tongs for handling hot foods, a meat thermometer, an oven thermometer, a spray bottle of water to extinguish flare-ups and heavy gloves or pot holders.❖

PICNICKING

Picnicking is a delightful form of recreation enjoyed by people worldwide. Americans, and especially Californians, somehow seem to find more reasons and places to practice this art. They picnic in the mountains, at the seashore, in parks, in motor homes, on sand dunes, at sporting events, at open-air concerts—in fact, any place where a tablecloth can be spread. Even the tablecloth is not a necessity.

A few minutes of planning is perhaps the best assurance of an enjoyable picnic, devoid of disappointments, frustrations and that familiar quote, "I wish I had...." From a convenience and sanitation standpoint, it is far better to prepare as much of your picnic food as possible in your own kitchen. Conveniences are usually scarce at picnic sites.

Decide what foods will be served at each course. Unless you're sure of maintaining cold foods at about 40F (5C) or below, it is best to avoid foods high in protein and moisture. These include milk, cream, poultry, fish, shellfish, eggs, mayonnaise, cream pies and other such foods. These foods are especially susceptible to bacterial growth and can cause illness if not kept cool.

Select and wash containers in which foods or drink will be transported. Plan ways to keep hot items hot and cold items cold. Thermal bottles or jugs in 1-pint to 2-gallon capacity can be used to transport cold food or drink. These bottles should be chilled with ice water for at least 5 minutes. Pour out water and fill immediately with chilled food or drink. Close top securely.

An ice chest or cooler is most practical for transporting cold foods and bottled or canned drinks. All cold foods and drinks should be chilled in their containers in your refrigerator before being placed in an ice chest. Close lid securely. Refrigerants for ice chests include:

Ice Over Food Containers: Place chilled food containers with lids in chest. Pour ice cubes or crushed ice over containers. This is perhaps the most efficient method to ensure uniform cooling. But a word of caution—food containers must be tightly sealed to avoid water seeping in.

Ice & Salt Mixture: An empty 3-pound coffee or shortening can filled with ice and salt makes an excellent refrigerant. Place a layer of ice cubes or a 1-inch layer of crushed ice in can. Sprinkle ice with two tablespoons salt. Continue layering alternately with ice and salt until full. Place lid securely on can. Place filled can upright on a piece of foil in center of ice chest and arrange cooled food containers around and on top of can.

Frozen Water-Filled Containers & Ice Substitutes: Water-filled containers can be empty milk cartons or similar containers that have been washed and filled with water to 1-1/2 inches from top. Seal with tape and freeze. Commercial ice-substitutes or nontoxic gels can be purchased at most supermarkets and frozen. Place these containers in your ice chest and arrange chilled food containers among ice containers.

Dry Ice: Dry ice or carbon dioxide is best used for keeping ice cream and other frozen desserts below 32F (0C). Dry ice can be purchased at some ice-cream and liquor stores and at most ice plants. It should be handled with gloves to avoid burns and should be wrapped in heavy paper. For best results, tape wrapped dry ice to inside lid of ice chest or place on top of frozen food. Do not inhale fumes.

To carry hot food to a picnic site, try to time the cooking so that food is done just prior to departure. Foods can be transported hot for several hours in the containers in which they were cooked. The container should have a tight-fitting lid and must be well insulated immediately after it is removed from the stove or oven. Using pot holders or gloves, wrap hot container first in two thicknesses of foil and then in at least five layers of newspapers. Secure wrapping with tape. Longer preservation can be achieved by placing the wrapped food container in an empty ice chest.

Food cooked in slow-cookers can be transported in the pot. To do this, set the slow-cooker on HIGH the last 15 minutes of cooking time. Unplug and wrap entire cooker with lid in two layers of foil and then at least five layers of newspaper. Secure wrapping with tape. Place wrapped cooker upright in a heavy grocery bag. Close the bag and tape. Keep cooker in an upright position while transporting.

Hot food can be transported to the picnic in a thermal bottle or jug. Bottle or jug should be preheated with boiling water at least 5 minutes. Pour out hot water and fill with hot food; close top.

Finally, select and pack condiments, garnishes, equipment and supplies. Except for perishables, most items can be packed in a picnic basket or sturdy box.❖

Barbecue Tips

A good temperature for charbroiling is 375F (190C). At this temperature, you can hold your hand at grill level about 3 seconds. A good temperature for smoke-cooking is 325F (165C). At this temperature, you can hold your hand at grill level about 5 seconds.

To give food a smoke flavor, use wood chips. Soak wood chips in water and sprinkle chips over hot coals. IT IS NOT RECOMMENDED TO USE WOOD CHIPS DIRECTLY IN A GAS GRILL AS IT MAY CLOG THE GAS JETS. If using wood chips with a gas grill, place soaked chips in an old stainless-steel pie pan or other shallow pan. Place pan on the lava rock in the grill. After grilling, discard wood ash from shallow pan. Refer to your grill-owner's manual for additional directions.

Teriyaki Pinwheels   *Photo on pages 2 & 3.*

Marinating flank steak in a teriyaki sauce tenderizes the meat.

1/4 cup soy sauce
2 tablespoons honey
1/2 teaspoon ground ginger
1/4 cup vegetable oil
2 tablespoons white-wine vinegar

1 garlic clove, crushed
1/8 teaspoon pepper
1 beef flank steak
10 medium mushrooms

In a small bowl, combine soy sauce, honey, ginger, oil, vinegar, garlic and pepper. Place flank steak in a 13'' x 9'' baking dish. Pour soy-sauce mixture over flank steak; cover and refrigerate 4 hours or overnight, turning meat at least once. Drain meat, reserving marinade. Using a sharp knife, cut 10 crosswise strips from steak. Roll a strip of meat around each mushroom. Secure with 1 or 2 wooden picks. Place on grill, about 4 inches above heat. Cook 3 to 5 minutes on each side, brushing with marinade several times. Makes 5 servings.

Spiced Barbecued Ribs

Precooking ribs promotes tenderness and also renders out fat to minimize flame-ups.

1 apple, peeled, cored, cut in chunks
3 tablespoons lemon juice
2 tablespoons honey
2/3 cup chutney, fruit pieces and juice
2 tablespoons chopped green onion
1/4 cup flaked coconut
1/4 cup peanut butter

1 teaspoon curry powder
1 (3-1/2- to 4-lb.) slab fresh
  pork spareribs
Salt and pepper
Sliced oranges for garnish
Sliced papaya for garnish

In a blender or food processor, puree apple, lemon juice, honey, chutney and green onion. Add coconut, peanut butter and curry powder; process until mixed. Sprinkle both sides of ribs with salt and pepper; brush both sides with apple mixture. Wrap ribs in 2 thicknesses of heavy-duty foil, turning end-flaps of foil up to prevent juice from leaking out. Punch several small holes in top of foil. When coals are hot, divide them in half; arrange in 2 rows about 8 to 10 inches apart. Place foil-wrapped ribs on grill about 4 inches above heat and between 2 rows of hot coals. Temperature at food level should be 325F (165C). Cover and cook 1-1/4 hours or until tender. Remove ribs from grill. Spread coals in a single layer. Remove ribs from foil; pat with paper towel to remove excess fat. Brush both sides of ribs with apple mixture. Place ribs on grill 4 to 5 inches above coals. Cook about 6 minutes on each side; turn and brush with sauce several times. Cut into serving pieces. Serve hot. Garnish with orange and papaya slices. Makes 5 to 6 servings.

Bacon-Wrapped Beef

A creative way to use everyone's favorite—ground beef.

2 eggs, slightly beaten
1 teaspoon Worcestershire sauce
1/2 teaspoon chili powder
2 teaspoons seasoned salt
1/2 teaspoon pepper
1/2 teaspoon garlic salt

1 small onion, minced
1/4 cup minced green bell pepper
1/4 cup minced celery
3 lbs. lean ground beef
1 lb. sliced bacon, room temperature

In a large bowl, combine eggs, Worcestershire sauce, chili powder, seasoned salt, pepper, garlic salt, onion, green pepper and celery. Add ground beef; mix well. Shape meat in a cylinder 3 to 4 inches in diameter and 10 inches long; set aside. Separate bacon slices; set 4 slices aside. On a work surface, arrange remaining bacon slices vertically, so that the edge of each slice slightly overlaps. Using 4 reserved bacon slices, place 2 slices, horizontally, on each of the right and left sides of the vertical bacon slices. The ends should overlap 2 to 3 inches of the vertical slices. Place cylinder of beef across center of bacon slices. Pull horizontal bacon slices up and over ends of beef. Pull ends of vertical bacon slices up and over beef, overlapping the ends at the top. Tie roll with string at 1-inch intervals along the length of the roll; then at 2-inch intervals from one end to the other. Place bacon-wrapped beef on a 325F (165C) grill, 4 to 6 inches above heat, directly over a drip pan. Cover and cook 30 minutes. Turn meat; cover and cook 30 minutes longer or until bacon is well done. Cut and remove string; slice meat. Makes 10 to 12 servings.

Barbecued Beef Roast

Using a meat thermometer ensures accuracy in determining doneness.

1 cup dry red wine
1/2 cup vegetable oil
1 garlic clove, crushed
1 teaspoon salt
1/2 teaspoon pepper
1 tablespoon grated onion

1/2 teaspoon dried leaf rosemary
1/2 teaspoon dried leaf thyme
1 (5- to 6-lb.) beef chuck clod roast,
    boneless beef cross-rib roast, or
    beef sirloin-tip roast

In a small bowl, combine wine, oil, garlic, salt, pepper, onion, rosemary and thyme. Place beef in a deep rectangular dish; pour wine mixture over beef. Cover and refrigerate 6 to 8 hours or overnight, turning occasionally. Drain beef, reserving marinade. Insert a meat thermometer in the center of the beef. Place on a 325F (165C) grill, 4 inches from heat, directly over a drip pan. Brush with marinade. Cover and cook 1 to 2 hours or until meat thermometer registers 140F (60C) for rare or 160F (70C) for medium. During cooking, brush roast with marinade about every 15 minutes. Let stand 5 to 10 minutes before carving. Slice beef crosswise. Serve hot or cold. Makes 8 to 10 servings.

 Tip

When barbecuing for an extended time, add charcoal briquets perdiodically.

How to Make Bacon-Wrapped Beef

1/Using your hands, shape ground-beef mixture in a cylinder, about 3 to 4 inches in diameter and 10 inches long.

2/Arrange bacon on a work surface so that edge of each slice slightly overlaps. Place 2 slices horizontally on each side.

3/Place beef on center of bacon. Pull horizontal slices up and over beef. Pull vertical slices up and over beef, overlapping ends at top.

4/Using string, tie roll at 1-inch intervals along length of roll. Also, tie at 2-inch intervals from one end to the other.

Charcoal-Broiled Chicken Breasts   *Photo on page 4.*

Serve with grilled corn-on-the-cob and a fresh-fruit salad.

4 chicken-breast halves, boned, skinned
1/3 cup vegetable oil
1/3 cup dry white wine
1 teaspoon dried leaf tarragon
1 tablespoon honey

1 teaspoon dry mustard
1 tablespoon soy sauce
1 teaspoon salt
1/4 teaspoon pepper

Using a meat mallet or heavy cleaver, slightly flatten chicken-breast halves. Place breasts in a small bowl. In another small bowl or a 2-cup measure, combine oil, wine, tarragon, honey, mustard, soy sauce, salt and pepper. Pour oil mixture over breasts; cover and refrigerate overnight. Drain chicken breasts, reserving marinade. Place breasts on grill 2 to 3 inches above heat. Cook 5 to 10 minutes, brushing with reserved marinade at least once. Turn breasts; brush with marinade. Cook 5 to 7 minutes longer or until lightly browned and firm to the touch. Serve hot. Makes 4 servings.

Variation

Substitute 4 chicken halves for chicken breasts. Cook 10 to 15 minutes on each side. Prepare twice as much marinade.

Smoked Barbecued Chicken

If you plan to make a sauce from drippings, remove drip pan before adding wood chips.

1/2 cup white wine
2 tablespoons butter or margarine
1/2 teaspoon seasoned salt

1/2 teaspoon dried leaf tarragon
1 (5-1/2- to 6-lb.) roasting chicken

In a small saucepan, combine wine, butter or margarine, seasoned salt and tarragon. Cook over low heat until butter or margarine is melted; set aside. Soak 1-1/2 cups wood chips in 1 cup water, if desired. Truss chicken; place on a 325F (165C) grill, breast-side up, about 4 inches from heat and directly above a drip pan. Baste chicken with wine sauce. Cover and cook 50 minutes, basting with sauce every 10 to 15 minutes. Sprinkle wet wood chips over hot coals every 10 minutes throughout cooking time, or place chips in a shallow pan and place on the lava rock in gas grill, if desired. After 50 minutes, carefully remove drip pan, if drippings are to be used for a sauce. Cover and continue cooking and basting 30 to 45 minutes longer or until juices run clear when pierced with a fork between thigh and breast. Let stand 5 to 10 minutes before carving. Serve hot. Makes 4 servings.

Variation

For a light smoke flavor, use wood chips only during last 15 to 20 minutes of cooking.

Tip

Almonds in the shell will keep up to 6 months when stored in a cool, dry, well-ventilated place.

Smoked Duck à l'Orange

Leftover smoked duck adds a gourmet touch to salads and pizza.

2 tablespoons honey
1 teaspoon prepared mustard
1/2 teaspoon ground coriander

1/2 teaspoon salt
2/3 cup orange juice
1 (4- to 4-1/2-lb.) duck

In a small bowl, combine honey and mustard; stir until blended. Add coriander, salt and orange juice; stir until salt dissolves. Place duck in a loaf dish, pour orange-juice mixture over duck. Refrigerate 4 hours, turning duck at least once. Soak 1-1/2 cups wood chips in 1 cup water, if desired. Drain duck, reserving marinade. Truss duck; place on a 325F (165C) grill, breast-side up, about 4 inches from heat and directly above a drip pan. Brush duck with reserved marinade. Cover and cook 1 to 1-1/4 hours. Throughout the cooking time, sprinkle wet wood chips over hot coals every 10 minutes, or place chips in a shallow pan and place on the lava rock in gas grill, if desired. Baste duck with marinade throughout cooking time. Duck is done when juices run clear when pierced with a fork between thigh and breast. Let stand 5 to 10 minutes before carving. Serve hot. Makes 3 to 4 servings.

Variation

To use drippings from duck for sauce, cook 45 minutes without adding wood chips. Use tongs to tilt duck over drip pan to drain body cavity of juices. Carefully remove drip pan from barbecue. Cook 15 to 30 minutes longer, brushing duck with marinade and sprinkling wet wood chips on hot coals every 3 to 5 minutes.

Smoked Turkey

Smoke a large turkey—leftovers are great sliced and served cold in sandwiches.

1 cup white wine
1/4 cup butter or margarine
1 garlic clove, crushed
1 teaspoon seasoned salt

1 teaspoon dried leaf tarragon
1 (11- to 13-lb.) turkey
1/2 cup white wine

In a small saucepan, combine 1 cup white wine, butter or margarine, garlic, seasoned salt and tarragon. Cook over low heat, stirring until butter or margarine melts; set aside. Soak 1-1/2 cups wood chips in 1 cup water. Truss turkey; insert meat thermometer in thickest part of inner-thigh muscle. Pour 1/2 cup white wine into rear body cavity of turkey. Place turkey on a 325F (165C) grill, breast-side up, directly above a drip pan. Brush turkey with wine sauce. Cover and cook 3 hours or until meat thermometer registers 155F (70C), brushing with wine sauce at 10- to 15-minute intervals. Each hour during cooking time, add 6 to 8 briquets to fire, or enough briquets to maintain a temperature of 325F to 350F (165C to 175C) at food level. Remove drip pan if juices are to be used for making a sauce. Continue cooking turkey, brushing with any remaining sauce. Sprinkle wet wood chips over hot coals every 10 to 15 minutes until turkey is done, or place chips in a shallow pan and place on the lava rock in gas grill, if desired. When meat thermometer reaches 180F (80C), remove turkey from grill. Let stand 5 to 10 minutes before carving. Serve hot. Makes 12 to 14 servings.

Beach Seafood Cookout

A seafood cookout on the beach is an excellent way to celebrate. It's always an informal event that is sure to stimulate camaraderie. You'll need the following for cooking:

- A cement or ceramic fire ring; its rim should be at least 15 inches above the sand
- About 12 clay bricks
- A clean metal tub, 2-1/2 to 3 feet in diameter
- 15 to 18 wooden logs, 3 to 4 inches in diameter and about 2 feet long, plus paper or other kindling material
- A steamer basket or clean cloth bag
- Long tongs for handling hot food
- Pot holders
- 2 ice chests—one to hold seafood on ice, the other for iced beverages
- Card table(s) to hold food and service items

Next, you'll need the following foods:

- Dips and chips or other snacks
- Baking potatoes, double-wrapped in heavy-duty foil, 1 per person
- Hard-shell clams, 3 or 4 per person
- 1 to 1-1/4 lbs. live lobster, 1 per person
- Zucchini or crookneck squash, 1 per person
- 2 or 3 lemons, sliced, and 2 large onions, sliced
- Lemon wedges, 1 large wedge per person
- 3/4-inch butter pats, 1 per person
- Wine and or soft drinks, 1/2 bottle wine and or 1 to 2 soft drinks per person
- Bottled seafood sauce, if desired

For service equipment you'll need:

- Roll of paper towel, also use as napkins
- Knife and fork, 1 set per person
- Nutcracker and picks, about 1 per couple
- 14" x 8-1/2" metal tray and paper liner, 1 per person
- Glasses or cups, 1 per person

How to set up the cookout:

1/Inside fire ring, pile bricks in 2 vertical columns, about 18 inches apart, 18 to 20 inches from fire-ring wall. Stack to a height even with the rim of the fire ring.

2/Place empty tub on rim of fire ring and on top of both columns of bricks. Adjust brick columns to ensure tub's stability during cooking process.

3/Fill tub about 2/3 to 3/4 full of seawater. Include a handful of seaweed taken directly from the sea. Don't use dried seaweed found on the sand.

4/Place lemon slices and onion slices in water.

How to begin:

1/Start fire. When hot coals have accumulated in fire ring, place foil-wrapped potatoes around and just touching coals. At this point the meal should be ready in about 1 hour.

2/While waiting, serve wine or soft drinks and snacks.

After 25 minutes, water should be boiling; boil 20 minutes to sterilize.

3/Place clams in steamer basket or cloth bag; immerse in boiling water.

4/After 5 minutes, immerse lobsters, head first and upside down, in boiling water.

5/Wait an additional 5 minutes, then place zucchini or crookneck squash in boiling water.

6/In 6 to 7 minutes, all food in tub should be done and ready to eat. Remove tub and serve.

Slow-Smoked Fish

Large-boned fish, such as salmon, albacore and halibut, are ideal for smoking.

3 to 4 lbs. thick fish fillets,
  steaks or whole fish
1/4 cup salt
1 tablespoon sugar

1/2 teaspoon dried leaf basil
1/4 teaspoon dried leaf rosemary
1 tablespoon minced fresh parsley
2 quarts water

Clean and wash whole fish. In a large bowl or baking dish, combine salt, sugar, basil, rosemary, parsley and water; stir to dissolve sugar. Add fish; cover and refrigerate 4 hours, turning fish several times. Soak 3 cups wood chips in 2 cups water, if desired. Arrange hot briquets in a row along 1 side of firebox. Grease grill with oil. Place fish on side of grill that is opposite briquets. Cover and cook over low heat (about 200F, 95C at grill level) 3 to 5 hours depending on thickness of fish. Sprinkle wet wood chips on hot coals every 10 to 15 minutes, or place chips in a shallow pan and place on the lava rock in gas grill, if desired. Add 4 or 5 charcoal briquets to fire every hour. Fish will be done when firm but not hard to the touch and when juices no longer ooze from fish. Cut fish in serving portions or 1-inch cubes for appetizers. Serve hot. Or, serve appetizer portions, hot or cold, with wooden picks. Makes 5 to 7 servings or 50 to 60 appetizers.

Grilled Spiced Shrimp

They cook very fast, so watch carefully while grilling.

1/2 cup vegetable oil
1/4 cup red-wine vinegar
1 teaspoon crushed dried red peppers
1 teaspoon paprika

1 garlic clove, crushed
1/4 cup bottled barbecue sauce
1/2 teaspoon salt
1 lb. uncooked large shrimp, in shell

In a shallow bowl, combine oil, vinegar, red pepper, paprika, garlic, barbecue sauce and salt. Butterfly shrimp by cutting lengthwise down back, not cutting all the way through. Devein shrimp; do not remove shell. Marinate shrimp in oil mixture 1 hour or more. Soak a handful of wood chips in water about 15 minutes, if desired. Place wet wood chips on hot charcoal briquets, or place chips in a shallow pan and place on the lava rock in gas grill, if desired. Drain shrimp, reserving marinade. Thread shrimp on skewers, or place directly on grill. Cook about 2 minutes. Brush with marinade; turn and cook 2 to 3 minutes longer or until done. Makes 3 to 4 servings.

Skewered Sourdough Cubes   *Photo on pages 2 & 3.*

Serve each person an individual skewer of bread.

1/2 (16-oz.) loaf unsliced sourdough bread
3/4 cup butter or margarine, melted
1/4 cup grated Parmesan cheese (3/4 oz.)

1 garlic clove, crushed
1/2 teaspoon seasoned salt
1/4 teaspoon paprika

Cut bread in 1-1/2-inch cubes. In a small bowl, combine butter or margarine, cheese, garlic, seasoned salt and paprika. Thread 4 to 5 bread cubes on each of 4 (12- to 14-inch) metal skewers. Brush cubes with butter or margarine mixture. Place skewers on grill about 4 to 6 inches above heat. Cook 1 to 2 minutes, turning on all sides to brown evenly. Serve warm. Makes 4 servings.

Barbecued Sausage Kabobs

Very simple to prepare.

1 (1-lb.) pkg. smoked Polish sausage
  (kielbasa)
2 large oranges
1 green or red bell pepper

1/4 cup apricot jam
1/2 teaspoon prepared mustard
2 teaspoons chili sauce
1/4 teaspoon Worcestershire sauce

Cut sausage in 1-1/2-inch crosswise pieces. Peel oranges. Cut in 1/2-inch slices; then cut each slice in half crosswise. Remove stem and seeds from pepper; cut in 1-1/2-inch squares. Arrange sausage pieces, half orange slices and pepper squares alternately on 4 (14-inch) skewers. In a small saucepan, combine jam, mustard, chili sauce and Worcestershire sauce. If jam contains large pieces of fruit, chop them in small pieces. Heat jam mixture, stirring until melted. Brush jam mixture over kabobs. Place kabobs on grill about 4 inches above heat. Cook 2 to 3 minutes or until sausage edges begin to brown. Brush with additional sauce. Turn and cook other side 2 to 3 minutes. Serve hot. Makes 4 servings.

Herbed Lamb Kabobs

Plan ahead so you have time to marinate lamb at least 4 hours before cooking.

1 cup vegetable oil
3/4 cup white-wine vinegar
1 tablespoon minced fresh parsley
1 garlic clove, crushed
1 teaspoon salt
1/2 teaspoon pepper

1 teaspoon sugar or honey
1/4 teaspoon dried leaf rosemary
1/4 teaspoon dried leaf thyme
2 lbs. leg of lamb, cut in 1-inch cubes
16 small white boiling onions
4 bacon slices

In a large bowl, combine oil, vinegar, parsley, garlic, salt, pepper, sugar or honey, rosemary and thyme. Add lamb cubes. Cover and refrigerate at least 4 hours or overnight. Peel onions; steam or parboil until nearly tender, but firm. Drain onions. Drain lamb, reserving marinade. Using 4 (14- to 16-inch) metal skewers, thread 1 bacon slice alternately between lamb cubes and onions on each skewer. Place kabobs on grill about 4 inches above heat. Cook 6 minutes. Turn, brushing with reserved marinade. Cook 4 to 6 minutes longer or until desired doneness. Serve hot. Makes 4 servings.

Beach-Bum Franks

A special treat at the beach, park or in your own backyard.

1 (1-lb.) pkg. frankfurters
1/2 cup chili sauce
3/4 cup pineapple juice

1 tablespoon honey
1 tablespoon prepared mustard

Make 3 or 4 shallow diagonal slits through each frankfurter; set aside. In a small bowl, combine chili sauce, pineapple juice, honey and mustard. Brush frankfurters with chili-sauce mixture. Cook over medium heat 5 to 10 minutes, turning and brushing 2 or 3 times. Spoon sauce over barbecued franks. Serve hot. Makes 5 servings.

Barbecued Hot-Dog Sandwiches

Kids of all ages will love these quick and easy sandwiches.

1 (1-lb.) pkg. frankfurters
2 tablespoons barbecue sauce
1 tablespoon sweet pickle relish
1 teaspoon prepared mustard

1/4 cup mayonnaise
1/2 cup shredded Cheddar cheese (2 oz.)
12 frankfurter buns, split

Chop frankfurters until about the size of peas. In a large bowl, combine chopped frankfurters, barbecue sauce, relish, mustard, mayonnaise and cheese. Spoon mixture on bottom half of each bun. Cover with top half of bun. Wrap each sandwich in a 12" x 9" piece of foil. Place foil-wrapped sandwiches on grill 10 to 15 minutes, turning 3 or 4 times. Or, place in a 350F (175C) oven 10 to 15 minutes. Serve warm. Makes 12 sandwiches.

Cheese-Stuffed Tomatoes   *Photo on pages 2 & 3.*

Tomatoes are California's most valuable vegetable crop.

3 large tomatoes, cut in halves
1/4 cup soft breadcrumbs
2 tablespoons butter or margarine, melted
1/2 teaspoon dried leaf basil
1/2 teaspoon salt

1/8 teaspoon pepper
1/2 cup grated Monterey Jack cheese
  (2 oz.)
1 tablespoon chopped fresh parsley

Scoop out center of each tomato half, leaving a 1/2-inch-thick shell. Chop scooped-out tomato pulp; set aside. In a medium bowl, combine breadcrumbs, butter or margarine, basil, salt and pepper. Stir in cheese and chopped tomato pulp. Fill tomato shells with breadcrumb mixture. Wrap each stuffed half in foil. Place on grill, stuffed-side up. Cook 10 to 15 minutes or until cheese melts. Remove foil; sprinkle with parsley. Serve hot. Makes 6 servings.

Barbecued Squash   *Photo on pages 2 & 3.*

Broil and serve squash when you're barbecuing a main-dish meat.

1/4 cup vegetable oil
3 tablespoons lemon juice
1/2 teaspoon salt
1/4 teaspoon pepper
1 garlic clove, crushed

1/4 teaspoon dried leaf rosemary, crushed
1/2 teaspoon Worcestershire sauce
2 zucchini
2 crookneck squash

In a small bowl, combine oil, lemon juice, salt, pepper, garlic, rosemary and Worcestershire sauce; stir until salt dissolves. Cut zucchini and crookneck squash in halves, lengthwise. Score cut-sides with 1/2-inch-deep diagonal cuts; place in a shallow baking dish, cut-side down. Pour oil mixture over squash; let stand several hours. Drain squash; place squash, cut-side up, on grill about 4 inches above heat. Cook 7 minutes; turn and cook 7 minutes longer or until tender when pierced with a fork. Serve warm with barbecued meat. Makes 2 servings.

Fish & Seafood

alifornia's coastal waters provide a haven for many kinds of fish and seafood. The many lakes and streams supplement this bountiful catch with entirely different species of fish.

FISH FILLETS

Popular fillets in fish markets are petrale sole, seabass, sanddabs or Pacific red snapper. Sometimes these same fish are known by different names. Pacific red snapper actually belongs to the Pacific rockfish family. Species of this family vary widely in color and marking. Both petrale sole and sanddabs are members of the flounder family, a flatfish. Because of their flat shape, cutting results in wide flat fillets. Other members of this group are Rex and Dover sole.

FISH STEAKS

Fish steaks include salmon, halibut and swordfish. Pacific salmon comes in five main varieties. Colors range from deep red to pale pink. King or chinook salmon is the largest. Next is the smaller red or sockeye. Silver salmon or coho is larger but not as big as the king. Pink salmon often ends up in a can. Chum or Keta, may be available fresh or canned. Halibut, a large flatfish is generally cut in steaks. Swordfish has a firm meat-like texture. Both are excellent broiled.

SPORTFISHING

Sportfishermen return from streams or lakes with trout or catfish. Ocean fishermen on boats out of California harbors catch bass, bonita, barracuda, mackerel and rockfish. The lucky ones hook an albacore, the aristocrat of the tuna family.

SHELLFISH

Dungeness crab is California's pride. Depending on the season, it's sold in markets either live or cooked, fresh or frozen. Spiny Pacific lobster is found in California waters and can be identified by the large tail in which all the meat is concentrated. Frozen lobster tails are available cooked or uncooked. Identify cooked ones by their bright-red shell and firm white flesh. Shrimp is prominent in many popular dishes. Save money by buying uncooked shrimp and prepare them in your kitchen.

BUYING TIPS

When purchasing fish or seafood, freshness is the key. Fish should be either refrigerated or frozen. For best flavor, eat it as soon as possible. When freezing fish, wrap in moisture-vapor-proof paper or place in heavy freezer bags. Thaw fish in the refrigerator. Whichever type you choose, remember the delicate flesh cooks quickly.❖

Crown O'Dill Halibut

Topping is slightly puffy when it comes out of the oven.

1/3 cup all-purpose flour
1/2 teaspoon salt
1/8 teaspoon pepper
4 or 5 halibut or swordfish steaks
1/2 cup dairy sour cream
1/2 cup mayonnaise

2 tablespoons finely chopped dill pickle
1 tablespoon finely chopped green onion
1 teaspoon dried dill weed
1 teaspoon lemon juice
1/4 teaspoon seasoned salt
1/3 cup grated Parmesan cheese (1 oz.)

Preheat oven to 350F (175C). Butter a 13'' x 9'' baking dish. In a pie plate, combine flour, salt and pepper. Dip both sides of each fish steak in flour mixture. Place steaks in buttered baking dish. In a small bowl, combine sour cream, mayonnaise, dill pickle, green onion, dill weed, lemon juice and seasoned salt. Spread sour-cream mixture over fish. Sprinkle fish with cheese. Bake 30 to 35 minutes or until fish flakes with a fork. Serve hot. Makes 4 to 5 servings.

Herbed Fish Fillets

Use a combination of fresh rosemary, basil, thyme and oregano instead of fines herbes.

1-1/2 to 2 lbs. Pacific snapper or
  rockfish fillets
1 cup chopped fresh mushrooms
2 tablespoons chopped fresh chives
2 tablespoons chopped fresh parsley

1/4 teaspoon fines herbes
1/2 teaspoon salt
1/8 teaspoon pepper
1 cup dry white wine
1 cup whipping cream

Place fish fillets in a large skillet. Sprinkle mushrooms, chives, parsley, fines herbes, salt and pepper over fish. Pour wine over fish. Cover and simmer 5 to 7 minutes or until fish flakes with a fork. Remove fish; place in a shallow baking pan. Preheat broiler. Add cream to liquid in skillet. Cook over medium-high heat 5 minutes or until liquid is reduced by about half. Pour reduced liquid over fish. Broil fish, 4 inches from heat, 1 to 2 minutes or until top begins to brown. Serve immediately. Makes 5 to 6 servings.

Crunchy Almond Fillets

Sole, flounder, Pacific red snapper and seabass are excellent choices for this recipe.

1/3 cup all-purpose flour
1/4 teaspoon salt
1/8 teaspoon pepper
1 egg, beaten
1/4 cup milk
1-1/2 cups soft breadcrumbs

1/3 cup finely chopped toasted almonds
1 tablespoon finely chopped fresh parsley
6 fish fillets (about 1-1/2 lbs.)
1/3 cup butter or margarine
Lemon wedges

In a pie plate, combine flour, salt and pepper. In a small bowl, combine egg and milk. In a second pie plate, combine breadcrumbs, almonds and parsley. Coat each fish fillet with flour mixture; then dip in egg mixture. Dip egg-coated fillets in crumb mixture. Melt butter or margarine in a large skillet. Sauté coated fillets in butter or margarine 3 to 5 minutes or until golden brown on both sides. Serve hot with lemon wedges. Makes 6 servings.

Oriental Fish Fillets

Teriyaki sauce gives an Oriental character to the fish fillets.

2/3 cup soy sauce
1 garlic clove, crushed
2 tablespoons vegetable oil
2 tablespoons brown sugar

1/4 cup lemon juice
5 or 6 fish fillets such as bass or
    rock cod
2 tablespoons toasted sesame seeds

Combine soy sauce, garlic, oil, brown sugar and lemon juice. Arrange fish in a shallow rectangular dish. Pour soy mixture over fish. Marinate 1 hour or more. Preheat broiler. Drain fish, reserving marinade. Broil fish, 3 inches from heat, 3 to 4 minutes on each side. Brush with marinade once during broiling. Sprinkle with sesame seeds. Serve hot. Makes 5 to 6 servings.

Halibut with Avocado Béarnaise

California is the leading producer of avocados.

1/2 cup Tarragon Vinegar, page 44
2 whole peppercorns
1/8 teaspoon dried leaf chervil
1 teaspoon chopped fresh parsley
1 tablespoon chopped green onion or shallots

6 halibut or swordfish steaks
3 egg yolks
3/4 cup butter, melted
1 tablespoon lemon juice
1 avocado, chopped

In a small saucepan, combine vinegar, peppercorns, chervil, parsley and green onion or shallots. Cook over medium heat until mixture is reduced by half; strain and cool mixture. Broil fish about 4 minutes per side. In top of a double boiler, place egg yolks and cooled vinegar mixture; place over hot but not boiling water. Beat egg yolks and vinegar mixture, gradually pouring in butter while stirring constantly, until mixture is thick and creamy. Pour egg-yolk mixture into a blender or food processor. Add lemon juice and avocado; process until smooth. Spoon sauce over broiled fish. Makes 6 servings.

Sole Véronique

If fillet of sole is not available, substitute a mild-flavored white fish.

6 sole fillets (about 1-1/2 lbs.)
1/2 cup dry white wine
1 cup water
3 unpeeled lemon slices
2 onion slices
1/2 teaspoon salt

4 whole peppercorns
1 bay leaf
1/4 cup butter or margarine
1/4 cup all-purpose flour
1 cup half and half
1 cup seedless green grapes

Place fish fillets in a large skillet. Add wine, water, lemon, onion, salt, peppercorns and bay leaf. Bring to a boil over medium heat. Cover and reduce heat; simmer 4 to 5 minutes or until fish flakes easily with a fork. Drain, reserving liquid. Place fish in a shallow baking dish; keep warm. Strain reserved liquid; return liquid to skillet and cook 5 minutes or until reduced by half. Preheat broiler. In a small saucepan, melt butter or margarine. Stir in flour; cook 1 minute. Add half and half and reduced cooking liquid. Cook until thickened, stirring frequently; add grapes. Pour off any liquid that has accumulated around fish. Spoon grape sauce over fish. Broil fillets, about 4 inches from heat, 1 to 2 minutes or until golden and bubbly. Serve hot. Makes 6 servings.

Mariner's Fish Roll-Ups

For a special treat, serve each roll-up with a topping of mashed avocado.

1 cup flaked cooked crabmeat or
   chopped shrimp
5 fillets of cod, sole or
   haddock (about 1-1/4 lbs.)
2 tablespoons vegetable oil
1/2 cup chopped celery
2 tomatoes, chopped

1 small onion, chopped
1 fresh or canned whole green chili,
   seeded, chopped
1/2 teaspoon salt
1/4 teaspoon garlic salt
2 tablespoons chopped fresh parsley

Spread crabmeat or shrimp down center of each fish fillet. Roll each fillet, securing with wooden picks; set aside. In a large skillet, heat oil. Add celery, tomatoes, onion, green chili, salt and garlic salt. Cover and cook over medium heat 5 minutes. Add rolled fillets. Sprinkle parsley over fish rolls. Cover and cook 6 to 8 minutes or until fish flakes with a fork. Serve on a platter or individual plates. Spoon vegetable sauce over fish rolls. Serve immediately. Makes 5 servings.

Abalone Steaks

A traditional dish that's hard to beat.

6 abalone steaks (about 1-1/2 lbs.)
1 egg
1 tablespoon water
1/2 cup fine dry breadcrumbs
1/4 teaspoon salt

1/8 teaspoon pepper
2 tablespoons butter or margarine
2 tablespoons vegetable oil
1 lemon, cut in 6 wedges

If abalone steaks are not tenderized by the fish market, pound them with a wooden mallet until they become limp. In a small bowl, beat together egg and water. In a pie plate, combine breadcrumbs, salt and pepper. Dip each tenderized steak in egg mixture and then in crumb mixture. Heat butter or margarine and oil in a large skillet. Fry steaks quickly until golden on both sides. Garnish with a lemon wedge. Serve warm. Makes 6 servings.

Golden State Avocado Boats   *Photo on Cover.*

Elegant first course for VIP dinner or luncheon salad plate.

3 avocados
1 tablespoon lemon juice
2 tomatoes, finely chopped
2 tablespoons chopped watercress
2 tablespoons fresh or
   canned diced green chilies, drained

1 cup cooked small shrimp or crabmeat
1/2 teaspoon salt
1/3 cup dairy sour cream or
   Fresh Herb Dressing, page 43
Pitted ripe olives

Cut unpeeled avocados in halves. Scoop out pulp, leaving a shell of peel; set aside. In a medium bowl, cut avocado pulp into bite-size pieces; toss with lemon juice. Add tomatoes, watercress, green chilies, shrimp or crabmeat and salt; mix well. Spoon avocado mixture into avocado shells. Place each filled avocado shell on a plate. Top with sour cream or herb dressing. Garnish each plate with olives. Makes 6 servings.

How to Make Mariner's Fish Roll-Ups

1/Spread shrimp over each fillet. Roll each fillet, securing with wooden picks.

2/Cover and cook 6 to 8 minutes or until fish flakes easily with a fork.

Seafood Medley

California shellfish include abalone, crab, oyster and shrimp.

1/3 cup butter or margarine
2 tablespoons chopped green onion
1 cup sliced fresh mushrooms
1/3 cup all-purpose flour
1/2 teaspoon salt
1/8 teaspoon pepper
1 pint (2 cups) half and half
1/4 cup dry white wine
1 lb. fillet of sole, cut in strips

6 oz. fresh or frozen crabmeat, flaked
1 (8-oz.) jar cooked artichoke hearts,
   drained, cut in quarters
1 cup shredded Monterey Jack cheese
   (4 oz.)
1 cup soft breadcrumbs
2 tablespoons butter, melted
2 tablespoons chopped blanched almonds

Preheat oven to 350F (175C). In a medium skillet, melt 1/3 cup butter or margarine. Add green onion and mushrooms; sauté until onion is soft. Stir in flour, salt and pepper. Add half and half and wine. Cook until slightly thickened, stirring frequently. Stir in sole, crabmeat, artichoke hearts and cheese. Heat until fish is cooked. Spoon into a shallow 1-1/2-quart baking dish. In a small bowl, combine breadcrumbs, 2 tablespoons melted butter and almonds. Sprinkle crumb mixture over fish mixture. Bake 20 to 30 minutes or until bubbly. Serve hot. Makes 6 servings.

Tip

Before cooking fish, rub the skin with a wedge of lemon for added flavor and aroma.

Cioppino

This favorite San Francisco seafood stew is a meal in itself.

1/4 cup vegetable oil or olive oil
1 onion, chopped
1 garlic clove, crushed
1 green bell pepper, seeded, chopped
1/4 cup minced fresh parsley
1 (28-oz.) can Italian-style tomatoes with
    juice, cut-up
1 cup water
1 (6-oz.) can tomato paste
1/2 teaspoon dried leaf rosemary
1/2 teaspoon dried leaf basil

1 teaspoon salt
1/4 teaspoon pepper
Dash hot-pepper sauce
2 cups dry red wine
12 hard-shell clams, in shell
1 lb. fresh seabass or snapper
1 lb. large raw shelled shrimp
1 cooked Dungeness crab, cleaned,
    cut in pieces
Hot garlic toast or sourdough bread,
    if desired

Pour oil in a Dutch oven or heavy 6-quart pan. Add onion and garlic; sauté until onion is soft. Add green pepper, parsley, tomatoes, water, tomato paste, rosemary, basil, salt, pepper, hot-pepper sauce and wine. Cook, covered, 30 minutes. Add clams; cook 10 to 15 minutes or until shells begin to open. Cut fish in 1-inch pieces. Add fish and shrimp. Cook 5 to 8 minutes or until fish is tender and clam shells are open. Add crab; cook until heated through. Ladle into a tureen or large soup bowls. Serve with garlic toast or sourdough bread, if desired. Makes 6 to 8 servings.

Pacific Clam Chowder

A hearty, California-style chowder, perfect for using Pismo clams.

2 bacon slices, chopped
1/4 cup chopped onion
1 celery stalk, chopped
1 fresh or canned whole green chili,
    seeded, chopped
2 tablespoons all-purpose flour
1-1/2 cups water
1 large potato, peeled, chopped

1 teaspoon salt
1/4 teaspoon celery salt
1/4 teaspoon dried leaf basil
2 (6-1/2-oz.) cans chopped clams
    with liquid
1 (7-oz.) can artichoke hearts, drained,
    cut in bite-size pieces
1-1/2 cups half and half

In a medium saucepan, cook bacon until almost done. Add onion, celery and green chili. Cook, stirring, 3 minutes. Stir in flour; add water, potato, salt, celery salt and basil. Cover and simmer 8 to 10 minutes or until potato is tender. Stir in clams, artichoke hearts and half and half. Heat to just below boiling point. Serve hot in a tureen or individual soup bowls. Makes 5 to 6 servings.

Tip
_____

While traveling between San Francisco and Sacramento, plan on eating at the Nut Tree in Vacaville. This beautiful restaurant features novel presentations and combinations of California foods.

Crabs

DUNGENESS CRAB

The Dungeness crab is one of the most highly prized delicacies in California. Visitors at San Francisco's Fisherman's Wharf view them in the food stands and often sample them in various recipes at nearby restaurants. Whole Dungeness crabs are impressive to see and eat, but often intimidating to those who have not experienced the preparation.

Dungeness-crab devotees often prefer it in its simplest form—the main part of a meal. To enjoy this delicacy, start with only the freshest crab. If alive, pick up and hold the 2 back claws. Drop crab into a large pan of boiling salted water. Cover and simmer 15 to 20 minutes. Lift crab out of pan with tongs; drain and refrigerate about 2 hours.

Start with cooked whole crab from the fish market or grocery store or cooled crab you cooked. With your fingers or a knife, pry off hard top shell, known as the *apron*. Remove gills and spongy parts under shell; discard. Twist off claws at joints. With a sharp heavy knife, cut body into 4 pieces. For an impressive presentation, place cracked crab in a bowl of ice. Use a nutcracker and small picks to pull out every morsel of this delicacy. Dip crab into your favorite sauce. A popular California custom is to serve cracked crab with fresh sourdough bread and a glass of California wine. Count on 1 large Dungeness crab serving 2 people.

KING CRAB & SNOW CRAB

Although not a California product, Alaskan king crab and snow crab are quite popular here. The giant king measures as much as 6 feet from claw to claw. King crab is cleaned, cooked and frozen before being shipped to market. Because they are too large to be practical in their natural state, the legs are broken in segments or split lengthwise to make the meat more accessible. King crab can be cooked and served like Dungeness cracked crab. Broil the split legs and serve with a dipping sauce.

Snow crab is also cooked and ready to use when available in your market. You will see it in two different shapes—clusters which are parts of shoulder meat with parts of leg, or as claws with half the shell removed. Snow crab may be served cold, like other varieties, or heated by steaming or broiling. As the name implies, snow crab is filled with delicious white meat that is considered a delicacy.

Captain's Deviled Crab

If you like a more spicy flavor, increase hot-pepper sauce.

1/4 cup butter or margarine	1/8 teaspoon pepper
1 small onion, chopped	2 hard-cooked eggs, finely chopped
1/2 cup chopped celery	1/4 cup dry white wine
1/3 cup all-purpose flour	1 pint (2 cups) half and half
4 teaspoons prepared mustard	Dash hot-pepper sauce
1 teaspoon Worcestershire sauce	1 lb. crabmeat, cooked, flaked
2 tablespoons lemon juice	1/4 cup grated Parmesan cheese (3/4 oz.)
1/4 teaspoon salt	1/4 cup soft breadcrumbs

Preheat oven to 350F (175C). Melt butter or margarine in a large skillet. Add onion and celery; sauté until vegetables are soft. Add flour; cook 2 minutes, stirring constantly. Stir in mustard, Worcestershire sauce, lemon juice, salt, pepper, eggs, wine, half and half and hot-pepper sauce. Cook, stirring over low heat, until thickened. Add crabmeat. Spoon mixture into a 1-1/2-quart baking dish or 6 individual baking dishes. In a small bowl, combine cheese and breadcrumbs; sprinkle mixture over top. Bake 15 to 20 minutes or until bubbly. Serve hot. Makes 6 servings.

How to Open a Dungeness Crab

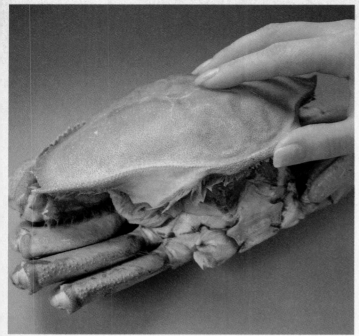

1/Pry off hard top shell known as the *apron*.

2/Use a sharp knife to cut body in quarters.

Hangtown Fry

This is one of many versions of a popular gold-rush-days dish.

8 bacon slices	1/8 teaspoon pepper
1 cup small oysters, shelled	1/2 cup finely crushed cracker crumbs
6 eggs	4 slices green bell pepper
2 tablespoons water	1 tomato, sliced
1/2 teaspoon salt	

In a large skillet, fry bacon until crisp. Remove bacon and drippings, reserving 3 tablespoons drippings. Drain oysters on paper towel. In a small bowl, combine eggs, water, salt and pepper. Dip drained oysters in cracker crumbs and then in egg mixture. Heat reserved bacon drippings in skillet. Add crumb-coated oysters; cook 1 minute on each side. Pour remaining egg mixture over lightly browned oysters. Cook over medium heat, lifting edges of cooked eggs to let uncooked part run underneath. Crumble cooked bacon slices; sprinkle over eggs. Garnish eggs with green-pepper and tomato slices. Makes 4 servings.

Mariner's Mold

Rich flavor is created by using two kinds of salmon.

1 (7-3/4-oz.) can salmon
2 tablespoons lemon juice
1 (.25-oz.) envelope unflavored gelatin
1/2 cup mayonnaise
3 oz. smoked sliced salmon, diced

1 teaspoon dried dill weed
2 tablespoons chopped green onion
1 cup whipping cream
Lettuce leaves
Fresh dill or green onions for garnish

Drain canned salmon, reserving liquid; discard bones and skin. In a small saucepan, combine reserved salmon liquid and lemon juice. Sprinkle gelatin over liquid mixture; let stand 5 minutes to soften. Cook over low heat, stirring constantly, until gelatin dissolves. In a blender or food processer, combine drained canned salmon, dissolved gelatin mixture, mayonnaise, smoked salmon, dill weed and green onion; blend until nearly smooth. Stir in whipping cream. Pour mixture into a 4-cup mold. Refrigerate 4 hours or until firm. Line a platter with lettuce leaves. Invert mold onto lettuce-lined platter. Garnish with fresh dill or green onions. Makes 4 to 6 servings.

Tuna Mousse

Serve this for your next salad buffet.

1/4 cup dry white wine
2 (.25-oz.) envelopes unflavored gelatin
1 cup chicken stock or bouillon
1/3 cup chopped celery
2 green onions, chopped
1/4 teaspoon salt
2 tablespoons sweet pickle relish, drained

1/2 teaspoon dried leaf marjoram
1/4 cup mayonnaise
2 (6-1/2-oz.) cans oil- or water-pack tuna, drained
1 cup half and half
2 egg whites
Lettuce leaves

Pour wine into a small saucepan. Sprinkle gelatin over wine; let stand 5 minutes to soften. Add stock or bouillon. Cook over low heat, stirring constantly, until gelatin dissolves; set aside. In a blender or food processor, combine celery, green onions, salt, pickle relish, marjoram and mayonnaise. Process 2 to 10 seconds. Mixture should not be pureed. Add dissolved gelatin mixture, tuna and half and half. Process 2 to 5 seconds to break tuna chunks apart. In a large bowl, beat egg whites until stiff, but not dry. Fold tuna mixture into beaten egg whites. Spoon into a 5-cup mold. Refrigerate 4 to 6 hours or until firm. Arrange lettuce leaves around edge of a medium tray or round platter. Invert mousse onto lettuce-lined tray or platter. Especially good for salad buffet. Makes 6 to 8 servings.

Tip

For a colorful garnish, fill center of ring mold with cherry tomatoes.

Poultry & Eggs

$\mathbf{C}$hicken holds a respected position on tables in practically every portion of the world, including California. It delights sophisticated palates as well as those with a preference for humble cooking.

Versatile chicken lends itself to a broad range of dishes. One reason for the wide variety of dishes is the number of ways in which chicken is sold. For example, whole roasting chicken represents Sunday dinner to most of us. California-Style Roast Chicken teams rice with almonds, apricots and raisins—giving character to an otherwise ordinary meal.

CHICKEN PARTS

There are probably more cut-up fryers at the market than any other form of chicken. The variety of cut-up parts allows you to choose favorite pieces. Any of our recipes calling for a cut-up broiler-fryer may also be used for chicken breasts, thighs or whatever your preference.

Many stores offer chicken breasts, both with and without the bone. Although it's easier to handle boned chicken breasts, remember you are paying for that convenience. If you're a budget-watcher, buy bone-in chicken breasts and do the boning job yourself. Then, try our elegant Lemon-Tree Chicken. A delicate rich wine sauce makes budget-stretching a delicious pleasure.

When buying whole chickens or chicken parts, allow 3/4 pound per serving. In other words, a 3- to 3-1/2-pound chicken should serve four to five. If unable to use all the chicken at once, freeze it for later use.

TURKEY PARTS

Turkey is also available in parts. This is especially convenient for small families which are unable to use a large whole turkey. Sometimes there is a choice of uncooked, cooked and even smoked or barbecued turkey parts. If there's leftover cooked turkey, remove it from the bone and cut it in bite-size pieces. Measure it in 1- to 2-cup units. Package it in heavy freezer bags or freezer containers. Be sure to label it before freezing. The next time you need two cups of cooked chicken or turkey, it will be a simple matter of thawing.

EGGS FOR BRUNCH

Sunday brunch has become a weekly event in many homes. Often the flavors are borrowed from our Mexican neighbors. Impress your friends with either the showy Balboa Brunch or the hearty Baja Quiche. Add a big bowl of fresh fruit to complete the meal.❖

California-Style Roast Chicken

Fruit-studded stuffing gives a new flavor to chicken.

1-1/2 cups cooked white rice	1/8 teaspoon ground nutmeg
1/4 cup toasted slivered almonds	1/4 teaspoon celery salt
1/2 cup chopped dried apricots	2 tablespoons butter or margarine, melted
1/4 cup chopped raisins	1/3 cup chicken stock or bouillon
1 teaspoon salt	1 (3-1/2- to 4-lb.) roasting chicken

Preheat oven to 375F (190C). In a medium bowl, combine rice, almonds, apricots, raisins, salt, nutmeg, celery salt, butter or margarine and stock or bouillon. Place chicken, neck-side down, in a large bowl. Loosely fill body cavity with rice stuffing. Do not pack stuffing in chicken. Tie legs securely to the tail; twist wing-tips under back. Place chicken, breast-side up, on a rack in a shallow roasting pan. Cover chicken loosely with foil. Roast chicken 2 to 2-1/2 hours or until a thermometer inserted in inner-thigh muscle, registers 180F to 185F (80C to 85C). Remove foil during last few minutes of roasting time to allow chicken to brown. Spoon stuffing into a serving dish. Let chicken stand 10 minutes before carving. Makes 4 to 6 servings.

Golden-Glow Chicken

You can cook this on the grill for backyard entertaining.

1/2 cup orange marmalade	1 garlic clove, crushed
1/4 cup orange juice	2 (2-1/2- to 3-lb.) chickens,
1 teaspoon ground ginger	cut in quarters
1/2 teaspoon dry mustard	2 tablespoons butter or margarine, melted
1 tablespoon Worcestershire sauce	Salt and pepper

Preheat broiler. In a small bowl, combine marmalade, orange juice, ginger, mustard, Worcestershire sauce and garlic; set aside. Place chicken quarters on a broiler pan, skin-side up. Brush with butter or margarine; season with salt and pepper. Turn chicken over; brush other side and season to taste. Broil, about 6 inches from heat, 10 minutes, brushing chicken twice with glaze. Turn chicken over; brush with glaze. Broil 5 minutes longer. Brush with glaze again; broil 10 minutes or until tender. Serve hot. Makes 8 servings.

Sweet & Spicy Chicken

Easy to prepare and a welcome flavor change.

1 (3- to 3-1/2-lb.) chicken, cut-up	1 garlic clove, crushed
2 tablespoons honey	Salt and pepper
2 tablespoons Dijon-style mustard	2 tablespoons sesame seeds

Preheat oven to 350F (175C). Arrange chicken pieces in a single layer in a 13" x 9" baking pan. In a small bowl or 1-cup measure, combine honey, mustard and garlic. Brush honey mixture on chicken. Sprinkle salt, pepper and sesame seeds over chicken. Bake 50 to 55 minutes or until tender. Makes 4 to 5 servings.

Lemon-Tree Chicken   *Photo on page 74.*

For convenience, make ahead; broil immediately before serving.

8 chicken-breast halves, skinned, boned
1/4 cup all-purpose flour
1/4 cup butter or margarine
1 teaspoon salt
1/8 teaspoon pepper

1 teaspoon grated lemon peel
2 tablespoons lemon juice
2 tablespoons dry white wine
1/2 cup whipping cream
1 cup shredded Swiss cheese (4 oz.)

Coat chicken breasts with flour. Melt butter or margarine in a large skillet over medium heat. Add chicken breasts; brown in hot butter or margarine. Add salt, pepper, lemon peel, lemon juice and wine; simmer 5 minutes. Preheat broiler. Remove cooked chicken breasts from skillet; place in a 13" x 9" baking pan. Gradually stir whipping cream into sauce in skillet. Pour cream mixture over breasts. Sprinkle with cheese. Broil, about 4 inches from heat, until bubbly. Serve hot with sauce. Makes 4 to 8 servings.

Gilroy Garlic Chicken

Your guests will never guess that 20 garlic cloves are in this dish.

3 tablespoons butter
1 (3- to 3-1/2-lb.) chicken, cut-up
1/2 teaspoon salt
1/8 teaspoon pepper
20 garlic cloves, unpeeled
1/4 cup red wine

2 tomatoes, peeled, seeded, chopped
1 tablespoon chopped fresh parsley
1/4 teaspoon dried leaf thyme
1 cup chicken stock or bouillon
3 tablespoons butter

Melt 3 tablespoons butter in a large skillet. Add chicken pieces; brown on both sides. Season chicken with salt and pepper. Arrange garlic cloves between chicken pieces. Add wine, tomatoes, parsley and thyme. Cover and cook over low heat, 25 to 30 minutes or until tender. Remove chicken; keep warm. Add stock or bouillon to drippings and garlic. Cook over medium heat, uncovered, 10 minutes. Increase heat to high. Whisk in remaining 3 tablespoons butter, 1 tablespoon at a time. Remove from heat. Strain sauce, pressing as much mixture as possible through strainer with the back of a spoon. Serve sauce over chicken. Makes 4 to 5 servings.

Gilroy Garlic

During the last weekend of July, garlic becomes the center of interest in Gilroy, California. The local people, as well as visitors from far and wide, turn out for the Gilroy Garlic Festival. Competition is keen among many food booths on "Gourmet Alley" with an unbelievable variety of dishes featuring garlic. Topping the event is a garlic recipe contest and cook-off where lucky finalists show off their cooking skills.

How to Make Bits-of-Gold Cornish Hens

1/Using a knife or vegetable peeler, cut peel from kumquats.

2/Cut kumquat peel in matchstick-size pieces.

3/Strain kumquats, pressing pulp through a strainer.

4/Sprinkle cooked kumquat peel over hens.

Bits-of-Gold Cornish Hens

A little more work, but worth the extra effort.

2 cups fresh kumquats
1/2 cup hot water
1 cup sugar
4 Cornish hens, about 1-1/2 lbs. each
1/4 cup butter or margarine, melted
Salt and pepper

2 tablespoons corn syrup
1/2 teaspoon ground ginger
1-1/2 cups chicken stock or bouillon
2 tablespoons cornstarch
1/4 cup cold water or orange liqueur

Using a sharp knife or a vegetable peeler, cut strips of peel from kumquats. Cut peel in matchstick-size pieces; set peeled fruit aside. In a small saucepan, combine peel, hot water and sugar; bring to a boil. Reduce heat and simmer 10 minutes, stirring occasionally. Let stand until serving time. Preheat oven to 350F (175C). Cut hens in halves, lengthwise, through middle of back and breast. Place hen halves, cut-side down, in a shallow roasting pan. Brush halves with butter or margarine; season with salt and pepper. Bake 20 minutes. While hens bake, cut each peeled kumquat in quarters. In a small saucepan, combine kumquat quarters, corn syrup, ginger and stock or bouillon. Bring to a boil; reduce heat and simmer 15 minutes. Strain kumquats, pressing as much pulp through a strainer as possible, using the back of a spoon. Pour kumquat juice over partially cooked hen halves. Bake 20 to 25 minutes longer or until tender. Turn oven off; pour drippings from roasting pan into a small saucepan. Place roasting pan of hens back in warm oven to keep hens warm. In a small bowl, dissolve cornstarch in water or liqueur; add mixture to drippings. Cook over medium heat, stirring constantly, until thickened and translucent. Spoon sauce over hot hens. Sprinkle hens with cooked peel. Serve hot. Makes 8 servings.

Tip
_____

When using bouillon as a substitute for stock, you may want to reduce the amount of salt called for in the recipe.

Sesame-Barbecued Chicken

A different flavor combination for grilled chicken.

1/2 cup soy sauce
2 tablespoons sesame seeds
1 teaspoon sugar
1 green onion, chopped

1 garlic clove, crushed
1/4 cup vegetable oil
1/8 teaspoon pepper
1 (2-1/2- to 3-lb.)chicken, cut-up

In a blender or food processor, combine soy sauce, sesame seeds, sugar, green onion, garlic, oil and pepper. Process until mixture is nearly smooth. Arrange chicken pieces in a 13" x 9" baking pan. Pour soy-sauce mixture over chicken. Cover and refrigerate 2 to 3 hours, turning once. Preheat broiler or prepare grill. Drain, reserving marinade. Brush marinade on 1 side of each chicken piece. Place pieces on a broiler pan or on a barbecue grill, marinade-side toward heat. Broil or grill, 5 to 7 inches above heat, 20 to 25 minutes. Brush other side with marinade. Turn and broil or grill other side 15 minutes or until tender. Makes 3 to 4 servings.

Chicken Exotica

A different and tasty way to serve chicken.

1/4 cup all-purpose flour
1/2 teaspoon salt
1/2 teaspoon ground ginger
1 (3- to 3-1/2-lb.) chicken, cut-up
1/4 cup butter or margarine
1 small onion, chopped
2 bacon slices, chopped

1 teaspoon curry powder
1 tablespoon all-purpose flour
2 tablespoons applesauce
2 tablespoons flaked coconut
1 tablespoon ketchup
1/2 cup chicken stock or bouillon

In a plastic bag, combine 1/4 cup flour, salt and ginger. Place several pieces of chicken in bag; close bag and shake to coat chicken. Remove coated pieces; repeat until all pieces are coated. Preheat oven to 400F (205C). Melt butter or margarine in a 13" x 9" baking pan. Roll coated chicken pieces in melted butter or margarine. Place pieces, skin-side up, in pan; bake 20 minutes. While chicken bakes, sauté onion and bacon in a medium saucepan until tender; pour off fat and discard. Stir in curry powder, 1 tablespoon flour, applesauce, coconut and ketchup. Add stock or bouillon. Cook 5 minutes or until slightly thickened, stirring frequently. Remove from heat. Brush sauce over baked chicken; bake 20 minutes longer. Brush chicken a second time with sauce; bake 20 minutes longer or until tender. Serve hot. Makes 4 to 5 servings.

Rancho Chicken

A poultry stroganoff rather than the usual beef version.

1/3 cup all-purpose flour
1 teaspoon salt
1/4 teaspoon pepper
1/4 teaspoon paprika
1 (3- to 3-1/2-lb.) chicken, cut-up
1/4 cup butter or margarine
1/2 teaspoon dried leaf tarragon

1 cup chicken stock or bouillon
3/4 cup dry white wine
2 green onions, sliced
1/4 lb. mushrooms, thinly sliced
 (about 10 mushrooms)
1 cup dairy sour cream
Hot cooked rice

In a plastic bag, combine flour, salt, pepper and paprika. Place several pieces of chicken in bag; close bag and shake to coat chicken. Remove coated pieces; repeat until all pieces are coated. In a large skillet, heat butter or margarine. Over medium-low heat, brown chicken pieces on all sides. Add tarragon, stock or bouillon, wine and green onions. Cover and simmer 30 minutes. Stir in mushrooms and sour cream. Heat, stirring until blended. Serve with rice. Makes 4 to 5 servings.

Turkey-Stuffed Pita Bread

A great way to use extra turkey or chicken.

1 cup chopped cooked turkey or chicken
1 orange, peeled, cut in bite-size pieces
1 cup finely shredded cabbage
1/4 cup whole-cranberry sauce

1/4 cup chopped walnuts
1/4 teaspoon salt
1/3 cup mayonnaise
4 pita bread rounds

In a medium bowl, combine turkey or chicken, orange, cabbage, cranberry sauce, walnuts, salt and mayonnaise. Open each pita bread. Fill each pita with turkey or chicken mixture. Serve immediately. Makes 4 servings.

How to Make Baja Quiche

1/Sprinkle cheese over tortillas. Top with refried beans.

2/Garnish with tomato and avocado slices and cilantro.

Baja Quiche

If you're hesitant about spicy flavors, substitute regular pork sausage.

6 (6-inch) corn tortillas
2 cups shredded Monterey Jack
   cheese (8 oz.)
1 (8-oz.) can refried beans
1/2 lb. chorizo or Italian sausage,
   cooked, drained
2 tablespoons canned diced green
   chilies, drained

2 eggs
1 pint (2 cups) half and half
1/2 teaspoon salt
1 avocado, sliced
1 tomato, sliced
Cilantro for garnish

Preheat oven to 325F (165C). Line a 9-inch pie pan with overlapping tortillas, extending about 1/2 inch over pan edge. Sprinkle half the cheese over tortillas. Top with layers of beans, chorizo or sausage and green chilies. In a small bowl, beat eggs; stir in half and half and salt. Pour egg mixture over chilies. Sprinkle remaining cheese over egg mixture. Bake 30 to 40 minutes or until firm. Top with avocado and tomato. Garnish with cilantro. Serve warm. Makes 5 to 6 servings.

Balboa Brunch

A complete brunch entree, similar to Eggs Benedict.

1 eggplant, unpeeled
1 teaspoon salt
2 tablespoons butter or margarine
1 small onion, chopped
2 tomatoes, peeled, seeded, chopped
1/2 teaspoon salt

1/8 teaspoon pepper
1/2 teaspoon dried leaf basil, crushed
1 cup chopped cooked ham
1/3 cup vegetable oil
6 eggs
Fresh basil leaves for garnish

Cut eggplant in 6 crosswise slices. Sprinkle 1 teaspoon salt over slices; let stand 30 minutes. Melt butter or margarine in a skillet over medium heat. Add onion; sauté until soft. Add tomatoes, 1/2 teaspoon salt, pepper, basil and ham. Simmer 5 minutes. Remove from heat; keep warm. Rinse and drain eggplant; pat dry with paper towel. Heat oil in a large skillet over medium heat. Add eggplant; fry in hot oil 5 to 8 minutes or until browned and tender. Remove from heat; keep warm. In a small saucepan, poach eggs. Place 1 poached egg on each slice of cooked eggplant. Spoon tomato mixture over eggs. Garnish with basil. Serve immediately. Makes 6 servings.

Egg & Olive Brunch Bake

If available, fresh corn gives added flavor.

6 eggs, beaten
1/2 cup half and half
2 cups well-drained whole-kernel corn
1 teaspoon Worcestershire sauce
1 teaspoon salt
1/2 teaspoon instant minced dried onion

1/2 cup sliced ripe olives
1 tablespoon chopped pimiento
1 (4-oz.) can diced green chilies, drained
2 cups shredded Monterey Jack or Cheddar
  cheese (8 oz.)

Grease an 8-inch square pan or a 2-quart casserole. Preheat oven to 350F (175C). In a large bowl, combine eggs, half and half, corn, Worcestershire sauce, salt, onion, olives, pimiento and green chilies. Stir in cheese. Pour egg mixture into greased pan or casserole. Bake 35 to 40 minutes or until center is firm and top begins to turn golden brown. Serve warm. Makes about 6 servings.

Ham & Cheese Bake

Start out with your preference of toasted or untoasted bread.

12 slices sandwich bread
2 tablespoons prepared mustard
6 (1/8-inch-thick) slices Monterey Jack
  cheese (about 8 oz.)
6 (1/8-inch-thick) slices cooked ham
  (about 6 oz.)

5 eggs
3 cups milk
1 teaspoon grated onion
1/2 teaspoon salt
1/4 cup canned diced green chilies,
  drained

Grease a 13" x 9" baking dish. Trim off bread crust. Spread 6 slices of bread with mustard. Arrange bread, mustard-side up, in greased dish. Top each piece with cheese and ham. Top with remaining bread. In a medium bowl, beat together eggs, milk, onion and salt. Stir in chilies. Pour egg mixture over bread. Cover and refrigerate 2 to 3 hours. About 30 minutes before baking, remove from refrigerator. Preheat oven to 325F (165C). Bake, uncovered, 1 hour. Serve hot. Makes 6 servings.

North-of-the-Border Huevos Rancheros

Serve refried beans on the side.

2 tablespoons vegetable oil
1 onion, chopped
1 green bell pepper, seeded, chopped
1 garlic clove, crushed
4 medium tomatoes, chopped
1 (4-oz.) can diced green chilies, drained
1/2 teaspoon salt
1/8 teaspoon pepper

1/8 teaspoon ground coriander
6 eggs
1/2 cup vegetable oil
6 (6-inch) corn tortillas
1/2 cup shredded Monterey Jack cheese
  (2 oz.)
1 avocado, thinly sliced

Heat 2 tablespoons oil in a large skillet over medium heat. Add onion, green pepper and garlic; sauté until soft. Stir in tomatoes, green chilies, salt, pepper and coriander; cook 5 minutes. With back of a large spoon, form 6 wells in vegetable mixture. Break 1 egg into each well. Cover and cook to desired doneness. While eggs cook, heat 1/2 cup oil in a medium skillet. Fry a tortilla over medium-high heat until light brown; turn and fry other side. Drain on paper towel. Repeat with remaining tortillas. Place tortillas on individual plates. Place a cooked egg on each tortilla. Spoon vegetable mixture over egg. Sprinkle with cheese. Garnish with avocado. Makes 6 servings.

California Omelet for Two

A colorful dish with a Spanish accent!

1 large tomato, chopped
2 tablespoons canned diced green
  chilies, drained
1 tablespoon chopped green onion
2 tablespoons finely chopped celery
1/8 teaspoon salt
1 teaspoon minced fresh cilantro leaves

6 eggs
2 tablespoons milk or water
1/4 teaspoon salt
1/8 teaspoon pepper
1 tablespoon butter or margarine
1/4 cup dairy sour cream
6 avocado slices

In a small saucepan, combine tomato, green chilies, green onion, celery, 1/8 teaspoon salt and cilantro. Bring to a boil; reduce heat and simmer 3 minutes. Keep warm until ready to use. In a small bowl, combine eggs, milk or water, 1/4 teaspoon salt and pepper. Beat with a fork or whisk until blended. In a 9-inch omelet pan, heat butter or margarine over medium heat; pour in egg mixture. With a spatula, lift edges as eggs set; slightly tilt pan for uncooked mixture to run under cooked portion. Shake pan to loosen omelet. Remove from heat. Spoon warm filling over half of omelet. With spatula, fold other half over top of filling. Garnish with sour cream and avocado slices. Cut in half and serve on individual plates. Makes 2 servings.

Desserts

A bountiful supply of California fruits and nuts inspires good cooks to think of desserts throughout the year. Although shelled nuts and many fruits are in the stores year-round, seasonal fruits are more reasonable at the peak of production.

WINTER

Starting with the first of the year, citrus products reign supreme. It's the time of the year to bring a little sunshine into your life with Sunburst Orange Pie. With a rich and luxurious creamy filling in a crunchy crumb crust, this pie has a topping of orange sections and almonds. California navel oranges are perfect for this pie because they have no seeds and are easy to peel and section.

SPRING

Thoughts of spring bring visions of fresh strawberries. One of our favorite strawberry desserts is easy to prepare. Wash the berries, leaving the stems on. Drain them on paper towels or in a colander. Place them in a large glass bowl. Next to the strawberries, place a small bowl of dairy sour cream and a bowl of brown sugar. Let your guests pick up the strawberries, one at a time, dipping them in the sour cream and then sugar. Near our home, there's a roadside stand that occasionally has jumbo berries with long stems. Whenever possible, we buy these special berries for a dramatic dessert.

SUMMER

The sky is the limit for summer-fruit desserts. It's the season for melons as well as apricots, cherries, nectarines, plums and peaches. This is a great time to make a pie. You'll have trouble deciding whether to sample the sweet-tart taste of Sour-Cream-Nectarine Pie, Burgundy-Plum Tart with a wonderful Burgundy wine flavor or the elegant Glazed Peach Pie.

FALL

Apples, pears, pomegranates and persimmons dominate produce markets throughout most of autumn. It's the time of the year associated with nostalgic fragrances of cinnamon and ginger.

YEAR-ROUND

We realize that all irresistible desserts are not made with fruits. Many of them are chocolate, which is available any time. California's own Ghiradelli chocolate products have been made since Domingo Ghiradelli, unsuccessful in his search for gold, turned to the business which he knew best. One of the most elegant desserts is the El Capitan Cheesecake, every chocoholic's dream.❖

Gingered Fresh Figs

Fresh figs may be eaten with or without peel; it's strictly personal preference.

6 large fresh figs
1 (3-oz.) pkg. cream cheese,
  room temperature
2 tablespoons finely chopped walnuts
3 tablespoons sugar

1 tablespoon honey
2 teaspoons finely chopped
  crystallized ginger
1 unpeeled lemon, thinly sliced, seeded
1/3 cup water

Remove stems and cut figs in halves lengthwise. In a small bowl or 1-cup measure, combine cream cheese and walnuts. Top cut-side of each fig half with 1 teaspoon cream-cheese mixture. Place stuffed figs, cut-side up, in an 8-inch square baking pan; set aside. Preheat oven to 350F (175C). In a small saucepan, combine sugar, honey, ginger, lemon and water; bring to a boil. Reduce heat and simmer 5 minutes. Remove lemon slices; discard. Spoon sauce over stuffed figs. Bake 10 minutes, basting figs with sauce after 5 minutes of baking. Cool figs in pan 30 minutes at room temperature. Refrigerate figs until ready to serve. To serve, place 3 stuffed fig-halves on each of 4 dessert plates; spoon sauce over figs. Makes 4 servings.

Sliced Oranges Mexicana

A light fruit dessert with a touch of chocolate.

6 large navel oranges
1/4 cup powdered sugar
1 teaspoon unsweetened cocoa powder

1/4 teaspoon ground cinnamon
1/4 cup dairy sour cream, if desired

Peel oranges; cut each in 6 or 7 crosswise slices. Arrange on a plate or platter. In a small bowl, combine sugar, cocoa and cinnamon; sift sugar mixture over orange slices. Serve immediately, or cover and refrigerate until ready to serve. Top with sour cream, if desired. Makes 6 servings.

Fresh Plum Cobbler

At its best when served warm and fresh from the oven.

1/2 cup lightly packed brown sugar
1/4 cup all-purpose flour
1/4 teaspoon ground allspice
9 or 10 thinly sliced fresh plums
  (about 1-1/2 lbs.)
1/2 cup orange juice

1/2 cup all-purpose flour
1/3 cup granulated sugar
1/2 teaspoon baking powder
1 egg, slightly beaten
2 tablespoons butter or margarine, melted
Vanilla ice cream or dairy sour cream

Preheat oven to 375F (190C). In a large bowl, combine brown sugar, 1/4 cup flour and allspice. Add plums and orange juice; toss gently until blended. Spoon into an 8-inch square baking dish. In a medium bowl, combine 1/2 cup flour, granulated sugar, baking powder, egg and butter or margarine; beat until smooth. Drop flour mixture by tablespoonfuls into 6 to 8 mounds on top of plum mixture. Bake 35 to 45 minutes or until plums are tender and crust is golden brown. Serve warm with ice cream or sour cream. Makes 6 to 8 servings.

Lemon Mousse with Very-Berry Sauce

If raspberries are scarce, strawberries make a delicious substitute.

Lemon Mousse:

1/3 cup fresh lemon juice
1 (.25-oz.) pkg. unflavored gelatin
1 cup milk
1 teaspoon grated lemon peel
3 egg yolks

1/4 cup sugar
3 egg whites
1/4 teaspoon cream of tartar
1/2 cup sugar
1 cup whipping cream

Very-Berry Sauce:

1 teaspoon cornstarch
1/4 cup sugar
1/4 cup water
1 (10-oz.) pkg. frozen unsweetened
   raspberries or 1 pint fresh raspberries

1/4 cup strawberry liqueur or
   raspberry liqueur

Lemon Mousse:

Pour lemon juice in a small bowl. Sprinkle gelatin over lemon juice; let stand 5 minutes to soften. In a small saucepan, heat milk to about 175F (80C) or nearly boiling. Stir in softened gelatin and lemon peel; remove from heat. In a large bowl, beat egg yolks and 1/4 cup sugar until thick and creamy, about 5 minutes. Gradually beat in hot milk mixture. Pour egg mixture in saucepan. Cook, stirring constantly, over very low heat until mixture coats a metal spoon; set aside. In a medium bowl, beat together egg whites and cream of tartar until foamy. Gradually beat in 1/2 cup sugar. Beat until stiff, but not dry. Fold egg-white mixture into hot egg-yolk mixture. Refrigerate egg mixture while whipping cream. In a medium bowl, whip cream; fold into egg mixture. Spoon into 6 or 7 custard cups or individual molds. Refrigerate 3 to 4 hours or until firm.

Very-Berry Sauce:

In a small saucepan, combine cornstarch and sugar; stir in water. Add raspberries. Cook, stirring constantly, over medium heat until mixture is translucent and slightly thickened. Strain mixture, pressing pulp with the back of a spoon; discard seeds. Add liqueur. Refrigerate until ready to use. To serve, spoon about 2 tablespoons chilled sauce in bottom of 6 or 7 dessert dishes. Unmold each mousse onto sauce. Makes 6 to 7 servings.

Citrus-Pomegranate Compote

Crème de cassis is a liqueur made from black currants.

1 pomegranate, cut in half
1/4 cup sugar
3 tablespoons light corn syrup
2 tablespoons crème de cassis

2 grapefruit
2 oranges
Dairy sour cream

Using a teaspoon, scoop seeds from pomegranate halves; puree seeds in a blender or food processor. Strain pomegranate juice, discarding pulp. In a small saucepan, combine pomegranate juice, sugar and corn syrup. Cook, stirring constantly, over medium-high heat 2 to 3 minutes or until slightly thickened. Remove from heat; stir in crème de cassis. Set aside. Peel, section and seed grapefruit and oranges. In a small bowl, pour pomegranate sauce over citrus sections. Cover and refrigerate at least 1 hour. Serve fruit and sauce in a compote dish or individual sherbet glasses. Top with a dollop of sour cream. Makes 5 to 6 servings.

Snowcapped Pears

For a most impressive snowcapped look, top with lemon custard just before serving.

Pears:

8 firm pears	1 cinnamon stick
3 cups dry red wine	1 cup sugar
1 tablespoon julienned lemon peel	2 tablespoons cornstarch
2 tablespoons lemon juice	

Lemon-Custard Topping:

1/3 cup sugar	1 tablespoon lemon juice
1 tablespoon cornstarch	1/4 teaspoon grated lemon peel
1 cup milk	1/2 cup whipping cream
1 egg yolk, beaten	

Pears:
Peel pears, leaving stems attached. Cut a thin slice off bottom of pears so they will stand upright. In a 4-quart saucepan, combine wine, lemon peel, lemon juice, cinnamon and sugar; bring to a boil. Carefully place pears in boiling liquid. Cover and simmer 10 to 12 minutes or until pears are tender. Remove from heat; cool pears in syrup. Turn pears several times while cooling. When cool, remove pears and set aside; discard cinnamon. In a small bowl or cup, combine cornstarch and 1/2 cup wine syrup from cooking pears. Add cornstarch mixture to saucepan; cook, stirring constantly, over medium heat until thickened and translucent. Cool to room temperature.

Lemon-Custard Topping:
In a small saucepan, combine sugar and cornstarch; stir in milk. Cook, stirring constantly, over medium-low heat until boiling; remove from heat. Stir a small amount of hot mixture into egg yolk. Add egg-yolk mixture to hot sugar mixture in saucepan. Cook, stirring over medium-low heat, another 2 minutes. Stir in lemon juice and lemon peel; remove from heat and place plastic wrap on surface of custard. Cool to room temperature. In a medium bowl, whip cream; fold into custard. Stand a pear in each dish. Pour wine syrup over each pear. Top with custard topping. Makes 8 servings.

Kumquat Topping

An exciting flavor-surprise to spoon over ice cream, angel-food cake or waffles.

1/2 lb. fresh unpeeled kumquats, 18 to 20	1 cup sugar
1 cup orange juice	2 tablespoons orange liqueur, if desired

Cut each kumquat in 4 or 5 crosswise slices; discard seeds. In a medium saucepan, combine orange juice, sugar and kumquat slices; bring to a boil. Reduce heat and simmer 20 to 25 minutes or until mixture is a light-amber color. Stir occasionally while cooking. Remove from heat; add liqueur, if desired. Mixture thickens as it cools. Serve warm or cold. Makes 1-1/2 cups.

Tip

When pureeing fresh fruits for sauces, sorbets or mousses, remember that fully ripe fruit gives maximum flavor and ideal texture.

How to Make Glazed Oranges with Pistachios

1/Cut a thin layer of peel from oranges. Cut peel in matchstick-size strips.

2/Cut each orange in 1/4-inch slices. Secure each orange together with a wooden pick.

Glazed Oranges with Pistachios

Use a vegetable peeler to remove peel from orange.

5 oranges
1/2 cup sugar
2 tablespoons honey

1/2 cup water
1/3 cup orange liqueur
1/4 cup chopped pistachios or almonds

From each orange, cut a very thin layer of orange-colored peel. Be careful not to include any white part of peel. Cut in matchstick-size strips. In a medium saucepan, combine peel, sugar, honey, water and liqueur. Bring to a boil; simmer, stirring occasionally, until mixture is reduced and begins to thicken, about 10 minutes. Finish peeling oranges, being careful to remove all white part. Cut each orange in 1/4-inch crosswise slices. Put each orange back together, securing with a wooden pick. Place an orange in each of 5 individual dessert saucers, or place oranges in a medium glass bowl. Spoon sauce with peel over oranges; sprinkle chopped pistachios or almonds over oranges. Serve immediately. Makes 5 servings.

Tip
_____

For a satisfying dessert, sprinkle a little nutmeg and cinnamon over grapefruit halves. Bake 10 minutes.

Basic Pastry Shell

When measuring flour, spoon lightly into measuring cup, being careful not to pack down.

1-1/3 cups all-purpose flour	**1/2 cup shortening**
1/2 teaspoon salt	**3 tablespoons water**

In a medium bowl, combine flour and salt. Using a pastry blender or a fork, cut in shortening until all particles are size of small peas. Add water, 1 tablespoon at a time; toss with a fork. Work dough into a firm ball with your hands. On a lightly floured board, roll out dough to an 11-inch circle. Gently ease dough into a 9-inch pie pan. Trim dough 1/2 inch beyond edge of pan; fold under to make double thickness of dough around rim. Flute with fingers or fork. For a single-crust pie baked with a filling, bake according to directions for filling used. For a single-crust pie baked without filling, prick bottom and side of unbaked pastry with a fork; bake in preheated 425F (220C) oven 10 to 15 minutes or until golden brown. Makes 1 (9-inch) pastry shell.

Variation

Nut-Crust: Add 1 tablespoon finely chopped toasted almonds or walnuts to flour when making pastry dough.

Rich Tart Shell

Ideal pastry for miniature tarts.

1 cup butter, chilled	**1 egg, slightly beaten**
3-1/2 cups all-purpose flour	**1/4 cup vegetable oil**
1/2 teaspoon salt	**1/2 cup cold water**

Cut chilled butter in 1/2-inch slices. In a medium bowl, combine flour and salt. Using a pastry blender or a fork, cut in butter until all particles are size of small peas; set aside. In a small bowl, combine egg, oil and water. Using a fork, stir egg mixture into flour mixture until evenly distributed. Divide dough in half; shape in 2 balls. Wrap in plastic wrap or foil; refrigerate at least 1 hour. On a lightly floured board, roll out 1 piece of dough at a time to a 12- to 13-inch circle. For a large tart shell, carefully fit dough into a 11-inch quiche pan. For small tart shells, cut dough in 3-inch circles. Carefully fit dough into 2-inch tart pans or miniature muffin cups. For both sizes of tarts, trim edges even with tops of pans; prick side and bottom of each with fork. Bake all sizes of pastry in preheated 400F (205C) oven 10 to 12 minutes or until golden brown. Makes 40 (2-inch) tart shells, 24 (3-inch) or 2 (11-inch) tart or quiche shells.

Tip

Tart and pie shells may be blind-baked. This baking method lessens pastry shrinkage. To blind-bake a pastry shell, cut a square of foil larger than the pastry shell. Shape the foil to fit the shell. Evenly spread 1 cup dried beans in foil. Bake shell about 8 minutes. Remove beans and foil. Bake remaining time as indicated by the recipe. Be sure to keep these beans only for blind-baking pastry shells. Do not try to cook them.

Sunburst Orange Pie

If you don't have a 9-inch quiche pan, use a regular pie pan.

Graham-Cracker Crust:

1-1/4 cups graham-cracker crumbs
   (about 16 crackers)
2 tablespoons sugar

1/4 cup finely chopped almonds
1/3 cup butter or margarine, melted

Pie Filling:

1/3 cup sugar
2 tablespoons all-purpose flour
1 cup milk
3 egg yolks, beaten

1 (3-oz.) pkg. cream cheese, cut in cubes
1/4 teaspoon grated lemon peel
1/4 teaspoon almond extract

Orange Topping:

1/3 cup sugar
2 tablespoons cornstarch
1 cup orange juice

1 tablespoon orange liqueur, if desired
2 oranges, peeled, sectioned
10 to 12 toasted whole almonds

Graham-Cracker Crust:
Preheat oven to 350F (175C). In a medium bowl, combine graham-cracker crumbs, sugar, almonds and butter or margarine. Press crumb mixture onto bottom and side of a 9-inch quiche or tart pan. Bake 8 minutes. Cool crust while making filling.

Pie Filling:
In a small saucepan, combine sugar and flour; stir in milk. Cook, stirring constantly, over medium heat until mixture bubbles; simmer 2 minutes and remove from heat. Stir a small amount of hot mixture into egg yolks. Add yolk mixture to remaining hot milk mixture in saucepan. Cook, stirring, over low heat 2 minutes longer. Stir in cream cheese, lemon peel and almond extract; cool about 5 minutes. Pour mixture into baked crust. Refrigerate until firm.

Orange Topping:
In a small saucepan, combine sugar and cornstarch; stir in orange juice. Bring to a boil over medium heat, stirring constantly; simmer 1 minute longer. Add liqueur, if desired. Cool until sauce is warm to touch but not stiff.

To complete pie, arrange orange sections over filling in spoke-fashion around outside edge of pie. Spoon topping over orange sections. Arrange almonds at ends of orange sections in center of pie. Refrigerate 2 to 3 hours or until firm. Makes 1 (9-inch) pie.

How Much Citrus???

1 medium orange = 10 to 11 sections
               = 1/4 to 1/2 cup juice
               = 1/2 cup bite-size pieces
               = 3 to 4 teaspoons grated peel

1 medium tangerine = 8 to 12 sections
                 = 3 to 4 tablespoons juice
                 = 2 to 3 teaspoons grated peel

1 medium lemon = 2 to 3 tablespoons juice
              = 2 to 3 teaspoons grated peel

1 medium grapefruit = 10 to 12 sections
                  = 2/3 cup juice
                  = 3 to 4 tablespoons
                    grated peel

Sour-Cream-Nectarine Pie

Use cold firm butter or margarine for topping to get a good crumbly texture.

1 (9-inch) unbaked Basic Pastry Shell,
  page 135
1/2 cup granulated sugar
1/3 cup all-purpose flour
1/4 teaspoon ground nutmeg
1 cup dairy sour cream
1 egg, slightly beaten

5 cups sliced fresh nectarines
  (about 6 large)
2 tablespoons butter
2 tablespoons all-purpose flour
2 tablespoons lightly packed brown sugar
1/4 teaspoon ground cinnamon

Prepare Basic Pastry Shell. Preheat oven to 375F (190C). In a large bowl, combine granulated sugar, 1/3 cup all-purpose flour and nutmeg; stir in sour cream and egg. Add nectarines; stir to coat. Spoon mixture into unbaked pastry shell. Bake 20 minutes. In a small bowl, use a pastry blender or a fork to cut butter into 2 tablespoons flour, brown sugar and cinnamon; mixture should resemble coarse crumbs. Sprinkle butter mixture over top of hot pie. Bake 7 to 10 minutes longer or until topping melts and center is firm. Serve warm or cold. Makes 1 (9-inch) pie.

Burgundy Meringue Pie

Use a good-quality Burgundy for the best flavor.

1 (9-inch) baked Basic Pastry Shell,
  page 135
1-1/4 cups sugar
1/3 cup cornstarch
3 egg yolks, slightly beaten
1-1/4 cups Burgundy

3 tablespoons butter or margarine
2 tablespoons lemon juice
3 egg whites
1/4 teaspoon cream of tartar
6 tablespoons sugar
1/2 teaspoon vanilla extract

Prepare Basic Pastry Shell. Preheat oven to 350F (175C). In a medium saucepan, combine 1-1/4 cups sugar and cornstarch. In a small bowl or 2-cup measure, combine egg yolks and Burgundy; stir into sugar mixture. Cook, stirring constantly, over medium-low heat until mixture thickens and begins to boil. Boil gently 1 minute; remove from heat. Stir in butter or margarine and lemon juice. Pour hot Burgundy mixture into pastry shell; spread evenly. In a small bowl, beat egg whites and cream of tartar until soft peaks form. Gradually beat in 6 tablespoons sugar; continue beating until stiff and glossy peaks form. Beat in vanilla. Spread beaten egg-white mixture over pie filling, carefully sealing meringue to edge of pastry. Bake 12 to 15 minutes or until meringue is golden. Cool on a wire rack away from any draft. Refrigerate until ready to serve. Makes 1 (9-inch) pie.

Tip
───────────────
When a recipe calls for lemon juice and peel, grate the peel first. Cut fruit in half and squeeze to remove juice. To obtain maximum juice, bring lemons to room temperature. Roll lemon between your hand and work surface before juicing.

Persimmon-Nut Pie

Very similar to a pumpkin pie.

1 (9-inch) unbaked Basic Pastry Shell,
   page 135
2 large persimmons
1 tablespoon lemon juice
2 eggs
1/2 cup lightly packed brown sugar

1/4 teaspoon ground nutmeg
1/2 teaspoon ground cinnamon
1 cup half and half
1/2 cup walnut pieces
Whipped cream, if desired

Prepare Basic Pastry Shell. Preheat oven to 400F (205C). Cut persimmons in halves crosswise; using a teaspoon, scoop out pulp. Puree persimmon pulp and lemon juice in a blender or food processor. In a large bowl, combine pureed persimmon mixture, eggs, brown sugar, nutmeg, cinnamon and half and half; beat until smooth. Pour into unbaked pastry shell. Sprinkle walnuts over pie filling. Bake 10 minutes; reduce heat to 350F (175C). Bake 20 to 25 minutes longer or until center is firm. Cool on a rack. Serve with whipped cream, if desired. Makes 1 (9-inch) pie.

Glazed Peach Pie

Fresh peach taste makes this a big hit.

1 (9-inch) baked Basic Pastry Shell,
   page 135
6 cups peeled, sliced peaches
   (8 to 9 peaches)
1 tablespoon lemon juice
3/4 cup sugar

3 tablespoons cornstarch
3/4 cup water
1/8 teaspoon almond extract
1 to 2 drops red food coloring
Whipped cream

Prepare Basic Pastry Shell. In a large bowl, combine peaches and lemon juice. Remove 1 cup peaches; mash with a fork or puree in a blender or food processor; set aside. In a small saucepan, combine sugar and cornstarch. Add water; stir until blended. Add mashed or pureed peaches. Cook, stirring constantly, over medium heat until mixture begins to thicken. Simmer, stirring constantly, 2 minutes longer; remove from heat. Add almond extract and food coloring. Arrange peach slices in baked pastry shell; pour cooked cornstarch mixture over top. Refrigerate pie 2 hours or until firm. To serve, top with whipped cream. Makes 1 (9-inch) pie.

Prospector's Pie

A crown of whipped cream may be added for an elegant touch.

1 (9-inch) unbaked Basic Pastry Shell,
   page 135
3 eggs
3/4 cup lightly packed brown sugar
1/2 cup butter or margarine, melted

1/2 cup chopped walnuts
1/2 cup chopped dates
3/4 cup flaked coconut
1 tablespoon lemon juice

Prepare Basic Pastry Shell. Preheat oven to 350F (175C). In a medium bowl, beat eggs; gradually beat in sugar. Add butter or margarine, walnuts, dates, coconut and lemon juice; combine well. Pour into unbaked pastry shell. Bake 30 to 35 minutes or until center is firm. Cool on a rack. Makes 1 (9-inch) pie.

How to Make Burgundy-Plum Tart

1/Arrange plum wedges, slightly overlapping, in circles over surface of tart.

2/Refrigerate tart before serving. To serve, cut in wedges.

Burgundy-Plum Tart

Fresh pear slices may be substituted for plums.

1 (9-inch) baked Basic Pastry Shell,
   page 135
3 large ripe plums
1 cup sugar
3 tablespoons cornstarch

2 egg yolks, slightly beaten
1-1/4 cups Burgundy
2 tablespoons butter or margarine
1 tablespoon lemon juice

Prepare Basic Pastry Shell. Cut each plum in half; remove pit. Cut each plum half in 8 wedges; set aside. In a medium saucepan, combine sugar and cornstarch. In a small bowl or 2-cup measure, combine egg yolks and Burgundy; stir into sugar mixture. Cook, stirring constantly, over medium-low heat until mixture thickens and begins to boil. Boil gently 1 minute; remove from heat. Stir in butter or margarine and lemon juice. Pour hot mixture into tart shell; spread evenly. On top of filling arrange 2/3 of plum wedges in a circle around outer edge of tart. Wedges should overlap and skin of wedges should face in same direction. Arrange 1/3 plum wedges overlapping in a smaller circle in center of tart. Skin of these wedges should face in the opposite direction to those wedges in larger circle. Refrigerate 1 hour or more. To serve, cut in wedges. Makes 1 (9-inch) tart.

Tip

Shelled nut meats can be kept frozen up to 1 year.

California Fruit Tarts

For impressive fruit tarts, here are a few of our favorite combinations. Mix and match our suggestions with your own, depending on availability of ingredients.

You will need the following to make 20 to 22 (2-inch) tarts or 11 to 12 (3-inch) tarts:
1/2 recipe Rich Tart Pastry, page 135
1 recipe Crème Pâtissière
Assorted fresh California fruits
Apricot or currant-jelly glaze, if desired

Crème Pâtissière

1/4 cup all-purpose flour	3 egg yolks, beaten
1/3 cup sugar	1 tablespoon butter
1 cup milk	1/8 teaspoon almond extract

In a medium saucepan, combine flour and sugar. Gradually add milk, stirring until smooth. Add egg yolks; cook, stirring over low heat, until thickened or about 3 minutes. Remove from heat. Stir in butter and almond extract. Cover with plastic wrap; set aside to cool. Spoon 2 to 3 teaspoons crème into each 2-inch baked and cooled tart shell or 1-1/2 to 2 tablespoons crème into each 3-inch baked and cooled tart shell. Makes enough for 20 to 22 (2-inch) tart shells or 11 to 12 (3-inch) tart shells.

Fruit Toppings for 2-inch Tarts:
Use small pieces of fruit for these miniature tarts. Favorite toppings include:
● 3 or 4 boysenberries or blackberries with 1 cantaloupe or honeydew-melon ball
● 3 or 4 green or Tokay grapes, halved, seeded, if necessary
● 1/2 or 1/3 of a fresh fig with a walnut half
● 2 sliced strawberries with 1 honeydew-melon ball
● 2 tangerine or Mandarin-orange segments with a thick slice of banana (especially good in winter when fresh fruit is limited)

Fruit Toppings for 3-inch Tarts:
Combine small pieces of fruit with larger slices for variety. Favorite toppings include:
● 4 or 5 slices peeled fresh peach with several honeydew-melon balls
● 6 half-slices kiwi with a whole strawberry
● 4 or 5 slices unpeeled nectarine or plum with green seedless grapes
● raspberries or strawberries with peach slices
● blueberries with an apricot half

Choice of Glazes:
● Heat together 1/2 cup apricot preserves with 1 tablespoon apricot juice, orange juice or peach brandy. Strain to remove pieces of fruit from glaze. Lightly brush glaze over fresh fruit in tarts.
● Heat together 1/2 cup red-currant jelly with 1 tablespoon raspberry juice, orange juice or orange liqueur. Lightly brush glaze over fresh fruit in tarts.

Tip

To prepare orange and grapefruit sections, use a sharp knife to remove peel. Remove all the white pith. Cut along both sides of each membrane. Lift out sections from center.

Sierra-Snow Lemon Cake

For a more snowy effect, top the frosting with untoasted coconut.

Lemon Cake:

2 cups all-purpose flour
1-1/2 cups sugar
3-1/2 teaspoons baking powder
1/4 teaspoon salt
1/2 cup shortening

1 cup milk
4 egg whites
1/2 cup flaked coconut
1/2 teaspoon grated lemon peel

Lemon Filling & Frosting:

3 eggs
1-1/4 cups sugar
3/4 cup butter
1/2 cup lemon juice

1 teaspoon grated lemon peel
1 cup whipping cream
1/4 cup toasted flaked coconut
Lemon slices

Lemon Cake:
Preheat oven to 350F (175C). Grease and flour 2 round 9-inch cake pans. In a large bowl, combine flour, sugar, baking powder, salt, shortening and milk. Beat on low until blended; then, beat on high 2 minutes. Add egg whites; beat 2 minutes longer. Fold in 1/2 cup coconut and lemon peel. Spoon into greased pans. Bake 30 to 35 minutes or until cake springs back when gently pressed with your fingertip. Let stand in pans 5 minutes. Turn cakes out; cool on racks.
Lemon Filling & Frosting:
In top of a double boiler, combine eggs, sugar, butter, lemon juice and lemon peel. Place over simmering water; cook, stirring frequently, 15 minutes or until mixture coats a metal spoon. Cool until mixture can be spread. Remove about 1-1/2 cups filling; set aside. To make frosting, whip cream in a medium bowl; fold remaining filling into whipped cream.
To complete cake, spread half of reserved filling on 1 cooled cake layer; top with second layer. Spread remaining filling to within 1 inch of edge of top layer. Spread whipped-cream frosting over sides of cake; then spread, or pipe with a large star-tip, frosting over edge of top layer. Sprinkle coconut over top edge of frosting. Garnish with lemon slices. Makes 1 (9-inch) layer cake.

Strawberry-Crown Cake

An updated version of a dessert reminiscent of old-fashioned strawberry shortcake.

2 pints strawberries
1/4 cup sugar
2 eggs
1 cup sugar
1 cup all-purpose flour
1 teaspoon baking powder

1/4 teaspoon salt
1/2 teaspoon grated lemon peel
1/4 cup butter or margarine, melted
1/2 cup milk
1 cup whipping cream

Clean strawberries; cut berries in halves. In a medium bowl, sprinkle berries with 1/4 cup sugar; set aside. Preheat oven to 350F (175C). Grease a 9-inch ring mold. In a large bowl, beat eggs; gradually add 1 cup sugar, beating until light and fluffy. Add flour, baking powder and salt; beat until smooth. Stir in lemon peel, butter or margarine and milk. Immediately pour into greased ring mold. Bake 30 minutes. Let stand in pan 5 minutes; turn out on a cooling rack. When cool, set cake on a large plate. In a medium bowl, whip cream; spoon about half of whipped cream into center of cake. Decorate outer base of cake with remaining cream. Arrange strawberries on cream around base and on cream in center of cake. Makes 8 servings.

Spicy Persimmon Cake

A delightful combination of flavors.

2 large persimmons
2 tablespoons lemon juice
1 teaspoon baking soda
1-3/4 cups all-purpose flour
1-1/2 cups sugar
1/2 cup vegetable oil
1-1/2 teaspoons baking powder

Lemon-Cream-Cheese Frosting:
1 (3-oz.) pkg. cream cheese,
  room temperature
1/2 cup butter or margarine,
  room temperature

1/2 teaspoon salt
3 eggs
1 teaspoon ground cinnamon
1/8 teaspoon ground cloves
1/2 teaspoon ground nutmeg
1/2 cup chopped raisins
1/4 cup chopped walnuts

1 (1-lb. box) powdered sugar
1/2 teaspoon grated lemon peel
2-1/2 to 3-1/2 tablespoons lemon juice

Preheat oven to 350F (175C). Grease and flour 2 round 8-inch cake pans. Cut persimmons in halves crosswise; using a teaspoon, scoop out pulp. You should have about 1 cup pulp. Puree pulp and lemon juice in a blender or food processor. In a large bowl, combine persimmon puree, baking soda, flour, sugar, oil, baking powder, salt, eggs, cinnamon, cloves and nutmeg; beat 3 minutes. Stir in raisins and walnuts. Pour mixture into greased pans. Bake 25 to 35 minutes or until a wooden pick inserted in center of cakes comes out clean. Cool cakes in pans 5 minutes. Turn cakes out on cooling racks. Cool completely.
Lemon-Cream Cheese Frosting:
In a medium bowl, combine cream cheese, butter or margarine, powdered sugar, lemon peel and 2-1/2 tablespoons lemon juice; beat until fluffy. Beat in additional lemon juice, 1 teaspoon at a time, until frosting reaches spreading consistency. Spread frosting between layers, then over top and sides. Makes 1 (8-inch) layer cake.

Sour-Cream-Almond Cake

A rich pound-like cake with almonds baked into bottom and sides.

2 tablespoons butter or margarine,
  room temperature
1/3 cup sliced almonds
1 cup butter or margarine, room temperature
3 cups granulated sugar
6 eggs
3 cups all-purpose flour

1/4 teaspoon salt
1/4 teaspoon baking soda
1 cup dairy sour cream
1/2 teaspoon vanilla extract
1/4 teaspoon ground nutmeg
Powdered sugar

Preheat oven to 325F (165C). Brush bottom and sides of a 10-inch tube pan with 2 tablespoons butter or margarine; sprinkle almonds in buttered pan so they stick to the side and bottom of pan. In a large bowl, beat together 1 cup butter or margarine and granulated sugar until fluffy. Beat in eggs, 1 at a time. In a medium bowl, combine flour, salt and baking soda. Add flour mixture alternately with sour cream to egg mixture, beating until smooth. Stir in vanilla and nutmeg. Spoon into buttered pan. Bake 65 to 70 minutes or until cake springs back when gently pressed with your fingertip. Let stand in pan 15 minutes. Loosen cake edges with a spatula. Turn cake upside-down on cooling rack. Sift powdered sugar over cooled cake. Makes 1 (10-inch) cake.

Apricot-Almond Torte

A very elegant dessert, perfect for any special occasion.

Cake:

3/4 lb. blanched almonds (about 2-1/4 cups)	6 egg whites, room temperature
6 egg yolks	1/4 teaspoon cream of tartar
3/4 cup sugar	1/4 teaspoon almond extract

Apricot Filling:

2 cups chopped dried apricots	1/4 cup water
1 (8-oz.) can crushed pineapple with juice	1/4 cup sugar

Chocolate Glaze:

1 cup semisweet chocolate pieces (6 oz.)	1/4 cup butter
2 teaspoons vegetable oil	

Cake:
Preheat oven to 300F (150C). Grease a 9-inch springform pan. In a blender or food processor, grind almonds until about the consistency of fine breadcrumbs. In a large bowl, beat egg yolks and sugar until thick and creamy, about 5 minutes. Stir in ground almonds. In a medium bowl, beat together egg whites, cream of tartar and almond extract until stiff but not dry; fold into egg-yolk mixture. Spoon mixture into greased pan. Bake 1 hour. Cool in pan. Remove sides of pan. Split cake in half, making 2 full layers.

Apricot Filling:
In a medium saucepan, combine apricots, pineapple, water and sugar. Simmer 5 to 8 minutes or until fruit is tender. Cool. Spread filling over 1 layer. Top with second cake layer.

Chocolate Glaze:
In a small saucepan, combine chocolate, oil and butter. Heat over low until chocolate and butter melt. Pour glaze over top of second cake layer; spread evenly, letting some glaze drip down cake sides. Makes 8 to 10 servings.

Almond-Peach Squares

Light and delicate chiffon-like cake tops fresh sliced peaches.

5 peaches, peeled, sliced	3/4 cup zwieback crumbs
2 tablespoons sugar	(about 9 slices, crushed)
2 teaspoons lemon juice	1/4 cup finely ground almonds
1/4 cup butter or margarine,	1/2 cup milk
room temperature	1/2 teaspoon grated lemon peel
1/3 cup sugar	3 egg whites
3 egg yolks	Whipped cream

Preheat oven to 350F (175C). Lightly grease a 9-inch square pan. In a medium bowl, combine peaches, 2 tablespoons sugar and lemon juice; set aside. In a large bowl, beat together butter or margarine and 1/3 cup sugar. Beat in egg yolks until smooth. Add zwieback crumbs, almonds, milk and lemon peel. In a small bowl, beat egg whites until stiff, but not dry; fold into zwieback mixture. Spoon peach mixture into greased pan; top with batter. Bake 25 to 35 minutes or until firm. Cut in 9 squares. Serve warm topped with whipped cream. Makes 9 servings.

Date-Nut Bars

These bars stay moist, thanks to the date filling.

1/2 cup butter or margarine	1/2 teaspoon baking powder
1/4 cup granulated sugar	1/4 teaspoon salt
1 cup all-purpose flour	1/3 cup all-purpose flour
1/2 cup lightly packed brown sugar	1 cup chopped dates
2 eggs, beaten	1/2 cup chopped walnuts
1/2 teaspoon vanilla extract	Powdered sugar

Preheat oven to 350F (175C). Lightly grease an 8-inch square pan. In a medium bowl, combine butter or margarine, granulated sugar and 1 cup flour. Using a pastry blender or a fork, combine ingredients until mixture resembles coarse crumbs. Press crumbs lightly on bottom of greased pan. Bake 15 minutes or until lightly browned. In a medium bowl, combine brown sugar, eggs and vanilla. Stir in baking powder, salt and 1/3 cup flour. Add dates and walnuts; spoon mixture over baked crust. Return to oven 15 to 20 minutes longer or until firm. Cool in pan. Sprinkle with powdered sugar. Cut into bars. Makes 16 to 20 bars.

Lemon-Snow Bars

Fresh lemon juice really makes the difference.

1-1/2 cups all-purpose flour	1/4 cup lemon juice
1/3 cup powdered sugar	3/4 teaspoon baking powder
3/4 cup butter or margarine	3 tablespoons all-purpose flour
3 eggs	Powdered sugar
1-1/2 cups granulated sugar	

Preheat oven to 350F (175C). In a medium bowl, combine 1-1/2 cups flour, 1/3 cup powdered sugar and butter or margarine. Using a pastry blender or a fork, blend until mixture resembles coarse crumbs. Press crumb mixture on bottom of a 9-inch square pan. Bake 15 to 20 minutes or until edge of mixture begins to brown. In a medium bowl, beat eggs with 1-1/2 cups granulated sugar until pale and fluffy. Mix in lemon juice; fold in baking powder and flour. Carefully spoon topping over baked crust. Bake 20 to 25 minutes or until firm. Cool in pan. Sprinkle with powdered sugar. Cut into bars. Makes 20 to 24 bars.

Tip

When cutting dried fruits into small pieces, use scissors instead of a knife. If fruits are unusually sticky, dip scissors in hot water. If fruits are to be added to a batter, dip scissors in flour to prevent fruit pieces from sticking together.

Fig Cookies

Homemade version of the ever-popular Fig Newton.

Fig Filling:
1-1/2 cups dried figs, finely chopped
3/4 cup water
1/2 cup orange juice

1/3 cup sugar
1/2 teaspoon grated orange peel

Cookie Dough:
1/3 cup butter or margarine,
   room temperature
2/3 cup lightly packed dark-brown sugar
2 eggs
1 teaspoon vanilla extract

2-1/2 cups all-purpose flour
2 teaspoons baking powder
1/2 teaspoon baking soda
1/8 teaspoon ground mace

Fig Filling:
In a medium saucepan, combine figs, water, orange juice, sugar and orange peel. Simmer 10 minutes or until figs are tender and mixture thickens; set aside until ready to use.
Cookie Dough:
In a large bowl, beat together butter or margarine and brown sugar. Add eggs, 1 at a time, beating until light and fluffy; add vanilla. In a medium bowl, combine flour, baking powder, baking soda and mace; add to butter mixture. Divide dough in thirds; wrap each third in plastic wrap. Refrigerate 2 hours.
To complete cookies, preheat oven to 350F (175C). Roll out 1 package of dough at a time to about 16'' x 4''. Place on a 17'' x 14'' baking sheet. Spread 1/3 of fig filling about 1 inch wide along one side of dough and about 1/2 inch from edge of that side. Brush water on edges of dough; then fold unfilled side of dough over the filled side. Press edges to seal. Repeat with remaining cookie dough and filling. Bake 18 to 20 minutes. Cool. Slice bars crosswise into 2-inch lengths. Makes 24 cookies.

Browned-Butter Apple Drops

Cookies that are moist, delicious and nutritious.

1/2 cup butter or margarine,
   room temperature
1-1/2 cups lightly packed brown sugar
1 egg
1/2 teaspoon ground cinnamon
1/4 teaspoon ground cloves
1 teaspoon grated orange peel
1/4 teaspoon salt

1 teaspoon baking soda
2 cups all-purpose flour
1/4 cup milk
2 cooking apples, peeled, finely chopped
1/3 cup butter or margarine
2 cups powdered sugar
2 to 3 tablespoons hot water
1/2 cup chopped walnuts

Preheat oven to 400F (205C). In a large bowl, beat together 1/2 cup butter or margarine and brown sugar. Beat in egg until fluffy. Add cinnamon, cloves, orange peel, salt and baking soda. Alternately add flour and milk, beating until smooth after each addition. Stir in apples. Drop tablespoonfuls of dough, about 2 inches apart, on a baking sheet. Bake 10 to 12 minutes or until almost no indentation remains after touching. Remove from oven; cool on racks. In a small skillet, heat 1/3 cup butter or margarine over medium heat until light-amber color. Remove from heat; stir in powdered sugar. Add enough hot water to make a thick glaze. Drizzle glaze over cooled cookies. Sprinkle with walnuts. Makes about 65 cookies.

How to Make Fig Cookies

1/Roll dough to 16" x 4". Spread 1/3 filling along one side.

2/Brush water on edge of dough along side of filling.

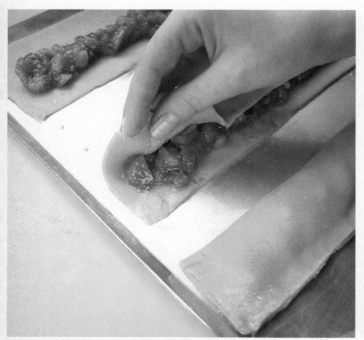

3/Fold unfilled side of dough over filled side. Press edges to seal.

4/Bake 18 to 20 minutes. When cool, slice bars into 2-inch pieces.

How to Make Oasis Stuffed Dates

1/Cut a slit the length of each date. Fill each date with peanut-butter mixture.

2/Dip 1 end of each stuffed date in melted chocolate. Cool on waxed paper until firm.

Oasis Stuffed Dates

Impressive gifts for friends or special treats for your family.

1/2 cup chunky peanut butter
1/2 cup powdered sugar
2 teaspoons butter or margarine, melted
1/4 cup flaked coconut

1/2 teaspoon grated orange peel
2 teaspoons orange juice
32 pitted dates
2 oz. sweet baking chocolate

In a medium bowl, combine peanut butter, powdered sugar, butter or margarine, coconut and orange peel; stir in orange juice. Cut a slit the entire length of each date, but do not cut date in half. Fill each date with about 1 teaspoon peanut-butter mixture. Melt chocolate over a pan of hot water or in a microwave oven. Dip 1 end of each stuffed date in melted chocolate. Cool on waxed paper or foil until chocolate is firm. Makes 32 stuffed dates.

Dates

If you are near Indio, California, during the middle of February, plan to spend a day in the area. The National Date Festival is held at that time. Date groves and date shops line the highway between Palm Springs and Indio. Enroute to the festival, taste and learn more about dates at the shops. At the festival, you'll see impressive displays of unbelievable varieties of dates and understand more about stages of date production.

Persimmon Pudding

A great moist steamed pudding.

Pudding:

1-1/2 cups all-purpose flour
1 cup granulated sugar
1 teaspoon baking powder
1 teaspoon baking soda
1/2 teaspoon ground allspice
1/4 teaspoon ground nutmeg
1/2 teaspoon salt
2 persimmons

1 tablespoon lemon juice
1/2 cup milk
1 egg
1/2 teaspoon vanilla extract
1/4 cup butter or margarine, melted
1/2 cup chopped raisins
1/4 cup chopped walnuts

Hard Sauce:

1/2 cup butter, room temperature
1 cup powdered sugar

2 tablespoons brandy

Pudding:

Grease a 6- or 8-cup mold. In a large bowl, combine flour, granulated sugar, baking powder, baking soda, allspice, nutmeg and salt; set aside. Cut persimmons in halves crosswise; scoop out pulp. Puree pulp in a blender or food processor. To flour mixture, add persimmon pulp, lemon juice, milk, egg, vanilla and butter or margarine; beat until smooth. Stir in raisins and walnuts. Spoon mixture into greased mold. Cover. Place on a rack in a steamer or 6- or 8-quart pot. Pour boiling water into steamer or pot until it comes half-way up the side of mold. Cover and steam 2-1/2 hours or until firm. Remove; let stand in mold 10 minutes. Invert to unmold.

Hard Sauce:

In a small bowl, beat together butter, sugar and brandy until smooth. Serve sauce over warm or cold pudding. Makes 6 to 8 servings.

Berry-Patch Kuchen

Up-dated version of old-fashioned berries and cream.

2 cups fresh or frozen unsweetened
  boysenberries or blackberries
2 cups all-purpose flour
1/2 cup sugar
1/2 teaspoon baking powder

1/2 cup butter or margarine
1/2 cup sugar
2 egg yolks
1 cup half and half

Thaw and drain berries, if frozen; set aside. Preheat oven to 400F (205C). In a medium bowl, combine flour, 1/2 cup sugar and baking powder. Using a pastry blender or a fork, cut in butter or margarine until mixture resembles coarse crumbs. Press flour mixture in bottom of a 9-inch round pan. Bake 20 minutes. In a small bowl, combine berries with 1/2 cup sugar. Spoon berry mixture over baked crust. In a small bowl, beat egg yolks with half and half. Pour egg-yolk mixture over berries. Bake 20 to 25 minutes. Serve warm. Makes 6 to 8 servings.

Tip

Walter Knott introduced boysenberries in 1935. They are a cross between the loganberry, blackberry and red raspberry. Today, Knottsberry Farm in Buena Park is world famous for its berry products.

El Capitan Cheesecake

Triple-chocolate spectacular designed for all chocoholics.

Chocolate Crust:
1-3/4 cups chocolate-cookie crumbs
   (about 30 thin chocolate wafers,
   crushed)

1 tablespoon sugar
2 tablespoons butter or margarine, melted

Filling:
4 oz. semisweet chocolate
2 (8-oz.) pkgs. cream cheese,
   room temperature
1 cup cottage cheese
1-1/4 cups sugar
3 eggs

1/2 teaspoon ground cinnamon
1/2 teaspoon vanilla extract
1 teaspoon instant coffee powder,
   if desired
1 cup whipping cream

Chocolate Topping:
1 oz. semisweet chocolate
1 cup dairy sour cream

2 tablespoons sugar

Chocolate Crust:
In a small bowl, combine cookie crumbs, sugar and butter or margarine. Press crumb mixture onto bottom and about 1-1/2 inches up side of a 9-inch springform pan. Refrigerate crust.

Filling:
Preheat oven to 350F (175C). Melt chocolate over hot water or in a microwave oven; set aside. In a large bowl, beat together cream cheese, cottage cheese and 1-1/4 cups sugar until smooth. Beat in eggs, melted chocolate, cinnamon, vanilla and coffee powder, if desired. In a medium bowl, whip cream; fold into cheese mixture. Pour mixture into chilled crust. Bake 65 to 70 minutes or until firm around outer edge. Center will not be quite firm. Turn off oven heat; leave cheesecake in oven with door ajar 1 hour. Remove from oven.

Chocolate Topping:
Melt chocolate over hot water or in a microwave oven. Stir in sour cream and sugar. Spread chocolate mixture over baked cheesecake. Refrigerate several hours or overnight. To serve, remove side of pan. Cut in wedges. Makes 1 (9-inch) cake or 12 servings.

Variation

For a smoother texture, place cottage cheese in a blender or food processor; process until smooth.

Tip
_____

To frost grapes, dip small clusters into slightly beaten egg whites. Sprinkle with granulated sugar. Set aside to dry. Use as a decorative garnish on a meat platter, fresh-fruit tray or molded salad.

Berry Bavarian with Lemon Crème

For elegant occasions, garnish with extra berries and whipped cream.

Bavarian:
2 cups fresh or frozen unsweetened
   boysenberries or blackberries
1/3 cup granulated sugar
1 (.25 oz.) envelope unflavored gelatin
1/4 cup water

2 tablespoons raspberry liqueur
2 egg whites
2 tablespoons powdered sugar
1/2 cup whipping cream

Lemon Crème:
1 tablespoon cornstarch
1/4 cup granulated sugar
1 cup milk

2 egg yolks, beaten
1/4 teaspoon grated lemon peel
1/2 cup whipping cream

Bavarian:
Thaw and drain berries, if frozen. In a blender or food processor, puree berries with juice and 1/3 cup granulated sugar. Strain berry mixture to remove seeds. Pour water in a small saucepan. Sprinkle gelatin over cold water; let stand 5 minutes to soften. Cook over low heat, stirring constantly, until gelatin dissolves. Stir gelatin mixture into berry puree. Add liqueur. Chill until syrupy. In a medium bowl, beat egg whites and powdered sugar until stiff but not dry. Fold into berry mixture. Whip 1/2 cup whipping cream; fold into berry mixture. Spoon into a 4- or 5-cup mold. Refrigerate until firm. Unmold on a platter or tray with a rim at least 1/2-inch high.

Lemon Crème:
In a small saucepan, combine cornstarch and 1/4 cup granulated sugar; stir in milk. Cook, stirring over low heat, until thick and smooth. Remove from heat; stir about 1/4 of the mixture into beaten egg yolks. Return mixture to pan. Add lemon peel; cook, stirring over low heat, about 2 minutes. Cool slightly. Whip 1/2 cup whipping cream; fold into egg mixture. Carefully spoon around mold on platter or tray. Serve Bavarian in individual dessert dishes. Top each serving with Lemon Crème. Makes 5 to 6 servings.

Golden State Crème Brûlée

Keep an eagle eye on these custards while they're under the broiler.

4 eggs
2 tablespoons granulated sugar
1 pint (2 cups) half and half,
   heated to about 150F (65C)

1/2 teaspoon vanilla extract
6 large strawberries, capped
1/3 cup sifted brown sugar

In top of a double boiler, beat eggs and granulated sugar until light and fluffy. Place over, but not touching, barely simmering water. Gradually add hot half and half while beating constantly. Heat, stirring constantly, until mixture coats a metal spoon. Remove from heat; add vanilla. Place a strawberry in each of 6 individual custard cups or baking dishes; pour in custard mixture. Refrigerate 6 hours or overnight. Preheat broiler. Before serving, sift brown sugar to about 1/4 inch thickness over each serving. Place custard cups or baking dishes in a 13" x 9" baking pan; surround with ice cubes or crushed ice. Broil 6 to 7 inches from heat until sugar forms a crust but does not burn, about 3 to 4 minutes. Makes 6 servings.

Kiwi-Strawberry Ripple Ice Cream

Swirl the strawberry mixture gently through the ice cream to give a marbled effect.

2 cups fresh strawberries or	**1/2 cup orange juice**
1 (10-oz.) pkg. whole frozen	**2 eggs**
strawberries	**3/4 sup sugar**
1/4 cup sugar	**1-1/2 cups whipping cream**
2 teaspoons cornstarch	**1/2 teaspoon vanilla extract**
1/4 cup light corn syrup	**6 to 8 drops green food coloring**
4 ripe kiwi, peeled, chopped	

In a blender or food processor, crush berries. In a small saucepan, combine 1/4 cup sugar and cornstarch. Stir in corn syrup and half the crushed berries. Cook, stirring constantly, over medium heat until thickened. Remove from heat and stir in remaining berries. Refrigerate until chilled. While chilling strawberry mixture, puree kiwi with orange juice in a blender or food processor. In a large bowl, beat eggs and 3/4 cup sugar 5 minutes or until thick. Stir in pureed kiwi mixture, whipping cream, vanilla and food coloring. Pour kiwi mixture into an ice-cream canister. Freeze in ice-cream maker according to manufacturer's directions. When frozen, remove lid and dasher from ice-cream canister. Instert a long metal spatula into center of ice cream. Slowly pull broad side of spatula toward edge of ice-cream canister. As you pull the spatula, pour reserved strawberry mixture into space created by moving spatula. Move broad side of spatula back and forth, 2 to 3 times, through ice-cream and strawberry mixture creating a marbled effect. Remove spatula. Cover canister with a double layer of waxed paper. Top with lid. Plug dasher hole with a cork or ball of foil. Ripen in brine according to manufacturer's directions or place canister in freezer to ripen. **Freezer method:** Pour prepared kiwi mixture into a 9-inch square pan. Cover with foil or plastic wrap. Place in freezer; freeze until almost firm, 1 to 3 hours. Spoon half of mixture into a large chilled bowl or chilled food-processor bowl. Beat with an electric mixer or metal food-processor blade until light and fluffy but not thawed. Repeat with remaining partially frozen mixture. Return to 9-inch square pan; freeze 30 to 45 minutes or until firm but not hard. Pour reserved strawberry mixture over frozen kiwi mixture. With a knife or metal spatula, swirl strawberry mixture through kiwi mixture to create a marbled effect. Return to freezer. Freeze 2 hours or until firm. Makes 2 quarts.

Gingered Melon Sorbet

Select a well-ripened melon for this cool tasty treat.

3/4 cup dry white wine	**1/2 teaspoon grated lemon peel**
1/2 cup sugar	**1 medium cantaloupe or crenshaw melon,**
2 tablespoons light corn syrup	**peeled, chopped**
1/4 cup minced crystallized ginger	**1 tablespoon lemon juice**

In a small saucepan, heat wine, sugar, corn syrup, ginger and lemon peel until sugar dissolves; cool slightly. In a blender or food processor, puree melon with lemon juice. Combine pureed melon and cooled wine mixture. Pour into an ice-cream canister. Freeze in ice-cream maker according to manufacturer's directions. **Freezer method:** Pour prepared mixture into a 9-inch square pan. Cover with foil or plastic wrap. Place in freezer; freeze until almost firm, 1 to 3 hours. Spoon half of mixture into a large chilled bowl or chilled food-processor bowl. Beat with an electric mixer or metal food-processor blade until light and fluffy but not thawed. Repeat with remaining partially frozen mixture. Serve immediately or return beaten mixture to pan; cover and freeze until firm, 1 to 2 hours. Makes about 2 quarts.

Pomegranate Jelly

During the short pomegranate season, make this jelly for year-round enjoyment.

4 large or 5 medium pomegranates
1 (3-fl. oz) foil pkg. liquid pectin

3-1/2 cups sugar
1 tablespoon lemon juice

Wash 5 (1/2-pint) jars in hot soapy water; rinse. Keep hot until needed. Prepare self-sealing lids as manufacturer directs. Cut pomegranates in halves. With a small spoon, scoop seeds into a food processor fitted with a plastic blade or a blender. Discard membrane and empty pomegranate shells. Process seeds until red pulp is off the seeds. Strain through 4 thicknesses of cheesecloth, pressing with the back of a spoon to strain as much liquid as possible. Discard seeds. Measure juice; there should be about 2 cups. Pour juice into a 6- to 8-quart saucepan. Open fruit-pectin pouch and stand, upright, in a cup or glass. Stir sugar and lemon juice into pomegranate juice. Bring to a boil over high heat, stirring constantly. Immediately stir in pectin. Stirring constantly, bring to a rolling boil that cannot be stirred down. Boil 1 minute, stirring constantly. Remove from heat. Using a metal spoon, skim foam from surface until surface is clear. Ladle hot jelly into 1 hot jar at a time, leaving 1/4-inch headspace. Wipe rim of jar with a clean damp cloth. Attach lid. Fill and close remaining jars. Invert jars 5 to 10 seconds. Then stand upright to cool. Or, seal with paraffin. Makes 4 to 5 (1/2-pint) jars.

Candied Orange Peel

Use as a garnish or serve as a snack or with fruit and cheese.

2 medium oranges
1/2 cup light corn syrup
1 cup sugar

1 cup water
Sugar

With a knife, cut orange peel into 6 sections. Remove peel from oranges in scored sections. In a medium saucepan, cover peel with water. Heat to boiling; boil 10 minutes. Drain. Repeat covering with water, boiling and draining 2 more times. After each cooking period, gently scrape off some of the soft white membrane with a spoon. Cut peel into 1/4-inch-wide strips. Combine corn syrup, 1 cup sugar and 1 cup water in a 2-quart saucepan. Stir constantly over medium heat until sugar dissolves. Add strips of orange peel. Bring to a boil. Reduce heat and simmer 45 minutes. Drain and cool. Roll strips in sugar. Arrange in a single layer on baking sheets. Let stand at room temperature about 24 hours. Makes about 1 cup.

Quick Tricks With California Fruits

- Transform dates or dried figs into tasty snacks or appetizers by stuffing with walnut halves, Cheddar-cheese cubes, pineapple chunks and coconut, or peanut butter and grated orange peel.
- For color and flavor, sprinkle fresh pomegranate seeds on fruit salads, sorbets or grapefruit halves.
- Freeze individual seedless grapes or small grape clusters on a tray. Serve several in a glass of white wine or clusters in a punch bowl.
- Fill cantaloupe halves with halved seedless grapes and half slices of kiwi. Top with plain yogurt and granola.
- To peel fresh peaches quickly, place in boiling water 30 seconds. Transfer immediately to cold water. Skins will slip right off.

Wines of California

The California wine industry is over 200-years old. The stature of these wines continues to grow abroad, as well as in the United States. Abundant sunshine and a diverse temperature range make it possible to grow virtually all wine-grape varieties in California. Over 500 California wineries are in operation and that number will, no doubt, continue to grow. California wine accounts for about 70% of the wine consumed in the United States. Other U.S. and foreign wineries supply the other 30%. There have been significant increases in the volume of California wine shipped to foreign countries in recent years. Retail value of California's wine production is over $4 billion annually, making it a significant segment of the state's economy.

WHAT'S IN A NAME?

The names of California table wines fall into two categories: *varietal* and *generic*. Varietal wine, by law, must be made from at least 75% of the named grape. If a wine's name includes the word Zinfandel, 75% of its juice content must have come from the Zinfandel grape. On the other hand, the name of a generic wine bears no relationship to the name of the grape from which the wine was made. Usually, a wine bearing a generic name is a blend of wines made from several different varieties of grapes without regard to varietal percentage. Generic wines are often labeled by color. However, certain semi-generic names are borrowed from European wine-growing regions, such as Rhine, Chablis or Burgundy.

SWEETNESS & COLOR

Table wine comes in three colors: *white, red and rose.* These wines generally fall in three levels of sweetness: *dry, off-dry or medium dry, and sweet.* Everything is relative, especially where the palate is involved. However, a sweet table wine is considered to be one with very noticeable sweetness. An off-dry table wine has a slight hint of sweetness, and a dry table wine imparts no detectable sweetness. The sweetness of sparkling wine or champagne is denoted in entirely different terms: *natural* (very dry), *brut* (dry), *extra dry* (very slight indication of sweetness), *sec* (noticeably sweet) and *demi-sec* (very sweet). Demi-sec is seldom made. ❖

How to Serve Wine

1/To serve white wine, chill bottle on ice to about 50F (10C). Serve with cheese and crackers.

2/Serve red wine at about 60F (15C). Especially good with grapes, nuts and pears.

Popular California Wines

RED VARIETALS	WHITE VARIETALS	ROSÉ VARIETALS
Barbera	Chardonnay	Cabernet Rosé
Cabernet Sauvignon	Chenin Blanc	Gamay Rosé
Gamay	French Colombard	Grenache Rosé
Grignolino	Pinot Blanc	Grignolino Rosé
Merlot	Grey Riesling	Zinfandel Rosé
Petite Sirah	White (Johannisberg) Riesling	
Pinot Noir	Sauvignon Blanc	
Zinfandel	Semillon	
	Sylvaner	
	Gewürztraminer	

RED GENERICS	WHITE GENERICS	ROSÉ GENERICS
Burgundy	Chablis	Vin Rosé
Chianti	Mountain White	Rosé
Claret	Rhine	
Mountain Red	Sauterne	

SELECTING & SERVING

In selecting wine for your enjoyment, it is both practical and proper that personal taste be your guide. For many years, we tried to select wine by trying those touted by wine experts. It finally occurred to us that our palates had not matured enough to appreciate the experts' recommendations. And, that we could judge what we like better than any expert. So, we took a different tack. We made it a point to try different kinds of wine offered by restaurants. We observed the names of wine served by our friends. We purchased wines that were offered as specials by local supermarkets and wine merchants. And, we periodically visited wineries to taste their products. Through these observations, we were able to find our favorite wines. Many of the wines we now enjoy are surprisingly inexpensive. Over the years, our preference for wine has changed significantly. Our first experiences with wine found us preferring the sweet ones; now our preference is toward dry wines.

In your quest for wine to pamper your palate, sample as many different wines as possible. In so doing, don't hesitate to ask the name of a restaurant's house-wine, or the name of the wine being served by your host. In your search, don't overlook California jug wine; it is an excellent value. Jug wine is table wine marketed in 1.5-, 3- and 4-liter jugs.

Most people prefer to drink white and rosé table wine chilled to about 50F (10C). When these wines are over-chilled, they lose much of their palate-pleasing qualities. Red table wine is best served at 60F (15C). Sparkling wine is generally served at 40F to 45F (5C). If it is necessary to chill a wine quickly, immerse the bottle in a container with equal parts ice and water. When using this method, white wine reaches drinking temperature in about 30 minutes, red wine in about 15 to 20 minutes and sparkling wine in 35 to 40 minutes.

At one time, it was traditional to serve sherry or vermouth with appetizers; red and dry rosé wine with cheese, chops, roasts, pasta and steaks; and white and medium-dry rosé wine with chicken, fish, egg dishes and other light dishes. Dessert wines, such as port, Marsala and Muscat, were served with cheeses, fruits, nuts and sweet pastries. This tradition is no longer in vogue. The right wine is the one you prefer.

COOKING WITH WINE

Alcohol in wine evaporates during the cooking process. Only the flavor of the wine is retained in the food. Some say to use the same wine in cooking as you drink. This, of course, will impart a highly satisfying taste to the food. However, if the wine you prefer to drink is an expensive one, it will likewise impart greater expense to the food. Perhaps it is best to compromise; that is, for cooking use a less-expensive wine that does have very favorable drinking qualities.

WINE-COUNTRY TOURS

A tour of the California wine country is an exceptionally pleasant and rewarding activity. Over 400 wineries are now open to the public. They offer wine for tasting and for sale. Wineries are located in 36 of California's 58 counties. No matter where you are in the state, a winery is not far away. A tour of the wineries has two distinct advantages: it offers an excellent opportunity to learn more about wine and it is an inexpensive pastime. Many facilities are open daily throughout the year; others are open only on specific days. Some require appointments to visit. The Wine Institute will be glad to send you a brochure that provides pertinent information on winery tours. Single copies of the brochure are available free of charge. Mail your request to: Wine Institute, 165 Post Street, San Francisco, CA 94108. Include a self-addressed envelope (at least 9-1/2" x 4-1/4") with enough first-class postage for a 2-ounce letter. Then enjoy planning and touring California's wine country.❖

Index

NOTICE: The information contained in this book is true and complete to the best of our knowledge. All recommendations are made without any guarantees on the part of the authors or HPBooks. The authors and publisher disclaim all liability incurred in connection with the use of this information.

9.346589143900